Clean Up On

Hero. Brother. Mentor. Advisor. Colleague. Dennis
has been all of these to me over the decades of my
ministry journey. Now, in the pages of this book,
he has become a "pastor to pastors." With
his extraordinary candor, wit and wisdom, Dennis
shares the practical realities of the journey with leaders
in the trenches of local church ministry. I'm incredibly
grateful he has captured his journey in this book,
confident it will encourage and empower every leader
who desires to serve Christ with excellence and
endurance.

Daniel Henderson
President - Strategic Renewal
www.strategicrenewal.com
National Director - The 6:4 Fellowship
www.64fellowship.com

Being an NFL coach, I don't have the good fortune of
consistently being part of a church community or
developing a relationship with the local Pastor during
an NFL season. Over the past thirteen years Dennis
Henderson has provided me with a mentoring
relationship which helps me to love and obey Jesus
Christ more, and to be the leader and pastor of my own
home to my wife and four children. Dennis not only
provides me with the spiritual guidance I need, but he
also provides a one of a kind relationship as a man of
integrity. I am a man seeking after God's own heart
with the help of my dear friend, Dennis Henderson.

Brett Maxie
Secondary Coach
Tennessee Titans

Clean Up On Aisle 2 is a book that is from the crucible of experience. Dennis Henderson knows the joys and challenges of being a pastor. This book puts into proper perspective the necessary balance of a pastor's life. In an age when pastor burn out and drop out is at an all time high, Dennis reveals to the reader what it takes to make it over the long haul. This is not a book written in theory. It is written by a man from the trenches that knows what he is talking about. He has and is living it out. This book is well worth your time. Sit back, relax, and enjoy the experience of *Clean Up On Aisle 2*.

Bobby W. Hancock, Pastor

Georgetown Baptist Church
Pottsboro, Texas

When Dennis was pastoring in the San Joaquin Valley in California, he went out of his way to befriend me. I didn't think I wanted to hang around a "Preacher Man", because my lifestyle was less than desirable. Dennis never judged me, but just accepted me for who I was. Later he discipled and mentored me in Christ Jesus. I highly recommend this book to any pastor who has a heart for the wayward. I will always be indebted to this godly man, as I am now living out my life serving my Lord and Savior.

Doug R. Haro
Retired Police Officer
Stockton California Police Department

Every leader has a story to tell; the story of this leader will pull you in and motivate you to live all out for Jesus. Working along side Dennis since 1996, I have had a front row seat to watching the story lived out.

Jeff Wideman, Ph.D
Executive Pastor
Fusion Bible Church
Sherman, Texas

Clean Up
On Aisle 2

by

Dennis Henderson

Monday Morning Press
DURANT, OKLAHOMA

Clean Up On Aisle 2

© Copyright 2013 by Dennis Henderson

Henderson, Dennis; 1947-
Clean Up On Aisle 2

1. Pastoral Care 2. Biography

Cover design: Chad Johnson & Joe Cavazos

Published by Monday Morning Press
49 Madison Avenue, Durant, OK 74701

To Billie

There is only one person to whom I could dedicate this book and that is my Billie, my gracious wife of 48 years. She has been my ministry partner from day one of ministry. Anyone who knows her well knows she is beyond the Proverb 31 woman. She has never disappointed me, always stood with me and has been my human encouragement through every experience in this book. Her walk with God has been my model. She is truly more precious than rubies.

Acknowledgements

Thank you to Connie Porter and Sharon Barker for doing a meticulous job proofing my work and allowing it to stay in the tone in which I wrote it. I appreciate Ken Myers for encouraging me to write, as I have always been hesitant to. His friendship and guidance in writing has been an immeasurable gift. Thank you to the staff of Sherman Bible Church for being committed to the cause of raising a church in an obscure North Texas town that has been used to have an impact for the Gospel.

Table of Contents

Foreword

Talk about a fish out of water. That is exactly how I felt when I started attending a weekly pastors prayer meeting hosted at a local Baptist church. I walked into the room, a bit hesitantly, and everyone was nice enough, but later some of the pastors admitted they weren't sure I was really a Christian. You see, I am an Anglican bishop, and everyone else in the room that morning was from Evangelical, Baptist, Bible Church or non-denominational backgrounds.

Dennis Henderson, who started the prayer meetings, wasn't there my first morning. I didn't meet him until a couple of weeks later, but even before meeting I had already figured out we were going to be cordial acquaintances at best. We were *so* different. He was Bible Church and I was Anglican. His background was pretty fundamentalist and I was anything but that. He pastored the biggest church in town and I pastored one of the smallest. We probably didn't agree on much anything theologically other than the absolutely bedrock things like who Jesus is and the doctrine of the Trinity. Oh - and he came to Texas by way of California - *California, mind you* - and I came to Texas by way of...well...by way of Texas.

So, why in the world am I writing a foreword for this man's book?

Because I met the guy and everything changed. At first I thought he was blowing smoke - talking about how his real focus wasn't just the local church he served, but the Kingdom of God in the area, that he cared for other pastors and congregations, that he wasn't in competition with others but wanted to help them. But over time, first months and then years, I saw that Dennis wasn't blowing smoke, he was the real deal. I saw him invest time and energy and finances into other pastors and congregations, I saw him make sacrifices in order to build up others, I saw him defer to fellow pastors when he could have basked in the limelight.

Dennis, though he wouldn't take credit for it if you asked him, spearheaded the endeavor to pull together local pastors into a unified whole. I've been pastoring for 35 years and have never seen anything like it. It started with the pastors meeting every Thursday morning for an hour of prayer; not chit-chat, not theologizing, not preaching, but real prayer. Added to our weekly prayer meetings came monthly times of learning ministry models and ideas from one another.

Eventually, as relationships strengthened among the pastors, we started meeting quarterly on Sunday evenings with our congregations joining together for a night of prayer and praise. Again, no long sermons (no sermons at all, in fact), no hidden agendas, just a little more than an hour of time when a thousand people from twenty or so different churches come together to worship Jesus and storm heaven with intercession.

The quarterly Sunday evening meetings led to "One Church." You'll hear more about it in the pages of this book, but in an effort to demonstrate to the world around us our unity in Christ, we started sharing pulpits, preaching common themes, plastering billboards and car windows with the message of "One Church, Many Congregations," and embracing joint ministry causes and opportunities such as members of our churches teaming together to help with tornado recovery in Oklahoma.

If you asked Dennis, he would say he wasn't the man responsible for all this, but I'm here to tell you it wouldn't have happened without him. God has set Dennis in our midst, here in the Texoma region, as a leader of leaders, a pastor of pastors.

Which brings me to the book you hold in your hands. I had the delight to read it as it was being written, and relished every chapter. It isn't a theological tome to convince you of a doctrinal position. It is, instead, two things. On the one hand it is a brief yet fascinating glimpse into Dennis' personal and ministry life, filled with stories from childhood through early ministry, from police work to leading large and successful congregations. On the other hand, it is a ridiculously wonderful and practical guide to pastoring, written by a man who has experienced it all - the good, the bad, and the ugly...and the often hilarious.

I could tell you I'm writing the foreword to this book because Dennis has shown himself to be a man's man, a pastor's pastor, and a forward thinking leader of the Church, but even that wouldn't tell the whole truth. Here's the real reason: because this fundamentalist-rooted, California sojourning, Baptist background, Bible Church pastoring, theologically different-than-me fellow has become a true friend.

There came a time in Jesus' relationship with his disciples when something changed, the relationship moved forward into something significantly different. They were no longer just disciples, no longer just servants, but he said to them, "I have called you friends."

Dennis and I call one another friends. We have spent a lot of time together on my back porch, talking about life and ministry and the Word of God. We have traveled together, we have shared ministry, he has endured my theological ramblings, and I thank God that we are truly friends, for that is a gift to be treasured more than gold.

I genuinely commend to you these wonderful pages written by my wonderful friend.

That is why in the world am I writing a foreword for this book.

Bishop Kenneth Myers
Church of the Resurrection
Sherman, TX

Introduction

If the teachers at my middle school were asked which students they thought would be a minister, my name would not be on the list. Never in their wildest imaginations, would they consider me as a prospect for ministry, any good will or holy calling. Now if they were asked which students could possibly end up in the penitentiary, I would have been at the top of a list for the first time. I had no hint of religion or righteousness in my life. I had never seen the inside of a church except the one time the Catholic lady next door took me to mass at six years old. I made it through the service, but on the way out, I was impressed that everyone was sticking their fingers in this little cup on the wall as they came in, were putting it on their foreheads and making some hand motions with it. I thought that must be pretty good stuff. So I took the cup off the wall on the way out. Some lady in a black outfit grabbed me and took the cup. She rambled on for what seemed like ten minutes. The only thing I remember her saying was, "Don't come back until you can act right." Well, that abruptly ended my first time to church. I knew I was not going to act right so I never went back. Now you have the summary of my church life up to twelve years of age. I look back and can't remember ever hearing the word "God" in our house outside of profanity. I had no knowledge of Noah, Moses, David, Goliath, Jesus or twelve disciples. I never saw a Bible. The whole God deal was a blank.

When a home was the forerunner of what has become known in recent years as a dysfunctional family, God surely was not around. By the time I was twelve, my mother had been married five times. When *Leave It to Beaver* came out on TV, it was like watching something from outer space. A mother and father, family dinners, and a happy family were never concepts to me.

I had no idea at six years old sitting in the back seat of a police car, snagged for vandalizing a car lot, that some day I would actually be in the front seat driving the police car. To say the least, my childhood days were colored as a troubled child. Principal offices, detention halls, and policemen, all painted the early days. Just as foreign as a family and a law-abiding citizen were to me, the concept of being a pastor was galaxies away. Notably it is incredible to know where God goes looking for His leaders. Thus, my path to ministry was not from thoroughbred stock.

This is my story of 46 years of trying to figure out what a pastor is all about. I have come to realize my name will never be alongside the mega church leaders of my time, but I have come to believe that every God-seeking, gospel-proclaiming pastor has great worth in God's vineyard. How does God measure success? Is it size, renown, or style that measures success? I am not sure; however, I suspect we might be surprised when the day comes and God evaluates and rewards our work. My work. I have enough to take care of right now. So I am not going to spend time trying to negatively evaluate pastors and churches. My plate is full. But I do want to go on record loudly for all pastors who are trying to stay in the race with integrity, commitment, faithfulness, and intensity. I have to assume I am in the final lap of the race. This lap is not only dedicated to a local pastorate, but to pastors. I do not consider myself a guru to whom they should listen in awe. I really don't have much to say. I am not a great thinker, philosopher or theologian. I do consider myself a cheerleader, friend, and one who has an incredible desire to see pastors run the race and not be disqualified. Possibly, the purpose of this season of my life is to encourage them and run as close as I can to them to catch their draft and finish well. Acts 20:24 comes to my mind almost daily. It is written in my heart, in the flyleaf of my Bible, and posted on my desk:

"However, I consider my life worth nothing to me, if only I may finish the race and complete the task that the Lord Jesus has given me — the task of testifying to the gospel of God's grace."

I write this mainly to pastors, but there is a possibility other leaders and Christ- followers in the church could be encouraged through my simple writing. You will find out I mean simple. I hope it is more like a conversation with you than a book.

I love being a pastor. Nothing else has ever consumed me or lured me. So I say with all my heart to you in the race, "It is worth it. We win at the end. Seeing the author and finisher of our faith will make every hurdle, stumble and injury worth it."

Chapter One
Clean Up On Aisle 2

It was 5:15 AM when my older brother Jim and I sat down on the corner in Lakewood, California, to begin our morning of rolling and then delivering newspapers. Many boys over the years have done that, but very few six year olds have done it. I was six. Jim had gotten the paper route and I was his tag along.

Eventually, I got my own route and peddled my bike down dark streets, dodging dogs that chased me and imagining all kinds of other scary things happening. The 7:00 AM stop at the donut shop to get a donut and hot chocolate was the every morning reward before hustling home to get ready for school. It cut into my profits, but the fifteen cents expense helped me survive this God-awful morning job. It was my first job. A work ethic was planted in my soul that would become my enemy years later. Paper routes, lawn jobs and shoe shining composed my early career in the work force.

Things moved up during the summer after 7th grade. I landed a job at a grocery store. Grocery store work was a dignified job. Ninety cents per hour to carry out groceries was much better than trying to collect money from newspaper customers in the evening. An apron, white shirt and tie were big stuff for me. Thanks to the work ethic my mother planted in me when she pushed me out the door for our paper routes, I was able to move up quickly in the grocery business. This was before unions enforced a bunch of rules. If you worked hard, which I did, you could attract the store manager's attention. I ran back in the store every time after placing groceries in customers' cars. I was getting a reputation as Mr. Hustle. I bugged the checkers every day to show me how the cash register worked. No scans in those days. You had to actually punch in the amount on the cash register, figure what one item that was marked 3 for 79 cents would cost, and memorize the produce prices. If you pushed hard enough and proved to them you could sack groceries faster than they could check them, the checkers started liking you. So it was four months later when the manager gave me a shot at checking. I passed up all the other bag boys. They were older and they were mad, but they were lazy. They were putting in time. I was looking at $2.10 per hour to check. So there I was checking.

Over the next few years, I moved through various positions in the store. I was put in the produce department for a while, then stocking, and finally to the best job... the meat department. Now the big money was coming in at $2.85 per hour. And I earned double time on Sunday afternoon when I came in to pull the case, deep clean and sanitize everything so that it was ready for Monday. Twenty-five hours a week and the Sunday pay put me in the highest income bracket of high school students in the work place. I was head and shoulders above babysitters, newspaper boys, and McDonald's workers. I loved grocery stores. Even today I inspect every grocery store I enter and think how I could improve it. To me there were not many unpleasant things about working in a grocery store. Now and then a customer got a little cranky, but overall, if you knew how to be friendly, compliment their kids, and ask, "How may I help you," then it was pretty easy.

As I look back, another thing I liked about the store work is that I walked out at the end of my shift and knew what I had accomplished. I could measure my aisle and know how many boxes of groceries I stocked on the shelves, see how much beef I had cut and placed in the meat locker case, and know how many boxes of produce I put out. I could close out my register drawer and know how many dollars of groceries I checked. My goal was always to check more groceries than the other checkers. An added bonus was when I went home, I didn't have to think about it again until I came the next day. Work was over that day.

The only thing I did not like was when that voice came over the loud speakers in the store and said, "Dennis, clean up on aisle 2." I hated hearing that. Aisle 2 was infamous. It was the aisle with most of the glass jars of jelly, mayonnaise, ketchup, syrup and everything else some kid or customer could drop. In addition, it seemed that on aisle 2, people would barf or kids would fill their diapers to overflowing. So when the speakers announced, "Dennis, clean up on aisle 2," I would dread going over there. It was always a mess to clean up.

Grocery work and ministry are quite a contrast. The things I liked about grocery work are not common to being a pastor, outside of "Clean up on aisle 2." Pastors hear that often, almost daily. The differences in the two jobs are recognizable to any pastor who has been in the ministry for any length of time. At the end of the day I can't measure the boxes, count the cash draw, look at the meat case or produce counters and think, "I nailed it today." Nope. I go home after work and wonder, "What in the world did I accomplish?" Plans I had that day were trashed with interruptions. I am sure many pastors resonate with me after a 12 to 14 hour day coming home and thinking, "I did not accomplish a thing today."

A long day with projects, sermons, and planning still hanging over my head would wear on me. To add to the frustration, when I got home, I didn't leave it at the office. It was still on mind as I tried my best to listen to kids tell me about school, boyfriends, and their activities. I would nod my head, as my wife would tell me about her day, yet my mind was trying to figure out tomorrow and how I could catch up. Then I would try to fall asleep for the few hours I had before my 6:00 AM men's discipleship group. Also, the budget meeting and the couple whose marriage is in the crapper would be coming tomorrow and I would be out of answers for them! Another "clean up on aisle 2" would be waiting for me tomorrow. Nothing was left at the office.

I read the books on boundaries, margins, and Andy Stanley's book on cheating on the church, but none of them seemed to be working. I'd wake up at 4:00 AM to get my quiet time in before I would head to the discipleship group. The day never seemed to have an end as it ran into the next day.

"Customers" in the church are not nearly as easy as those at the checkout line or meat case who asked for a thick T-Bone to be cut. I would always say, "Thanks for coming and come back soon." How many times have I wanted to say to the church consumer, "Why don't you not come back?" You pour out everything you have for them. You make sacrifices that God does not expect you to make for them. Then they expect more and some finally leave, criticize and do as much damage as they can on the way out. Their words are not always accurate or true, and they can cause doubt in the minds of those who stick with you. Only your personal integrity and commitment can stand up for you, and you hope it is strong enough to survive their venom.

I have to admit that some days I would like to hear over the loud speaker, "Dennis, clean up on aisle 2." Some days I have thought how easy it would be with my broom and mop getting aisle 2 cleaned up and getting back to my meat case, stocking my aisle and putting up the produce. I could go home and not worry about the job until tomorrow. Customers would seldom criticize my work or attack my character and motives. They would come back and smile when they saw me. I could measure the day and think, "I got my job done today."

Those days of foolish thinking have come over the course of forty-six years. However, I want to say as loud as I can, "There is nothing like hearing someone say, 'This is my pastor.'" I fully believe that being a pastor is the greatest privilege in the world. I look back without much complaint or any regret. I look back with amazement that I got to do this job and be paid for it. The very idea of helping people experience a forgiving Savior, discover a life with meaning, and salvaging something worse than "clean up on aisle 2" takes me through my final lap. Oh, yes, I need to say here that not all the church "customers" are cranky and self- centered. I have been blessed over the years, like many pastors, to have some of the most godly, selfless people in my churches. In truthfulness they outshone my walk with God and great will be their reward.

Why God would select a dysfunctional kid of 12, call him to represent Him, and sustain him year after year is a most confounding thought to me. I am grateful and humbled by this journey. I realize more than anyone how humanly unworthy I am to be a pastor. My only explanation comes from the words of Paul in I Corinthians 1:26-31:

For consider your calling, brothers: not many of you were wise according to worldly standards, not many were powerful, not many were of noble birth. But God chose what is foolish in the world to shame the wise; God chose what is weak in the world to shame the strong; God chose what is low and despised in the world, even things that are not, to bring to nothing things that are, so that no human being might boast in the presence of God. And because of him you are in Christ Jesus, who became to us wisdom from God, righteousness and sanctification and redemption, so that, as it is written, "Let the one who boasts, boast in the Lord."

"Clean up on aisle 2" fades quickly when compared to the high calling of a pastor. I do not know what your "clean up on aisle 2" is. Let me encourage you to never go back to aisle 2. It might be easier than your present post. It might be alluring to you at times, but I assure you the call of God trumps every other path you could choose today. Never wander over to your aisle 2, thinking it is better. What you do day after day in ministry counts for eternity. Remember your citizenship is not here. You, along with the thousands who have struggled to finish the race, are doing the most supreme work on earth.

Clean Up Assignment

I ask you to stop right now and reflect on the worthiness of your work. Do not measure it by others' work. It is your assignment, your most sacred privilege. God never planned for us to be carbon copies of each other. He loves diversity. So your first "clean up" assignment today is this:

Get quiet. Be still.

Ask the One who called you to speak softly to you about your call. Ask your Heavenly Father for a clear and fresh perspective of your calling. In this exercise do not look around to other ministries. Understand that your sovereign God has you where you are suppose to be for this moment. Do not focus on where you could be. Ask Him to help you focus on where you are now.

Take a moment to write in a journal or on your computer what a privilege and blessing it is to be His servant. Put aside your aisle 2 for now. Just focus on the great call He has given you.

Now, in writing, thank Him with a humble heart for allowing you to be in ministry.

Walk with me through the next chapters. I do not know on which lap you are in the race, but let's slow down for a while as we run and find refreshment together. I write as much for myself as I do for you. This writing is cathartic for me. It renews me in my final lap. My prayer as I write to you is that you will renew your call. Find encouragement that you run with a select group chosen for the most fantastic job on earth. A pastor. A leader.

Remind yourself often of the words of Jim Elliot in October 1949, *"He is no fool who gives what he cannot keep to gain that which he cannot lose."*

Chapter Two
Mom Got Saved!

In first and second grade after lunch everyone would line up and walk quietly back to the classroom. I would wait for "Miss Twist Your Tongue" and follow her down the hallway to the office area. For the next hour I would be in a small room for speech therapy. I still remember some of the exercises I had to do with my tongue and phrases she would have me repeat. I stuttered. I stuttered badly enough to be pulled out of class to help correct the problem. I did not understand fully what was going on, but I knew, along with many other things in my life, I was different than the other students. I have never really looked into what causes stuttering. I suspect it had something to do with my nervousness coming from my home situation. I really don't know. Like most things in life that seem to be a heartache or tragedy for me, I don't question it. I just move on.

I tell you about stuttering because I do public speaking every week. We call it preaching-teaching. I need to back up and tell you how I came into the public speaking arena. My mother raised me the first twelve years of my life. Her mother would live with us from time to time and, of course, a stepfather who I was suppose to call Dad for a year or two. By age twelve my mother had moved from being a waitress at a bar to selling cosmetics on the home party plan. She ran across a lady who was a Baptist preacher's wife with a capital B. I assume that the lady had her soul-winning antenna up when she met my mother. This lady took her purchase of cosmetics to another level. She took interest in my mother. Without a doubt the Holy Spirit alerted her to the lostness of my mother. Plus, this pastor's wife was a genuine soul-winner. After a few weeks of conversation and a home visit to share the gospel, my mother accepted Christ, was born again, and I mean… really saved! I could tell a difference in my mother immediately. All of the alcohol was poured down the drain. She was calm. Honestly, she actually looked different.

A few days later my mom was taking me to a building on the south side of town. It was a small fundamental Baptist church. This was now my second church experience. There was nothing on the wall to take home. In fact, there was nothing on the walls period. It was a simple cement block building with tiled floors. It was a box with metal folding chairs. There was nothing formal about that gathering. The most memorable part of the visit was the preacher up there yelling at me who kept pounding on this big wooden box. I thought he must have gotten up in a bad mood. I heard familiar words from home like "hell" and "damn." I did not understand what he was talking about with those words, as I could not connect with the word "soul." I kept looking at my shoes. I was thinking that there must be something wrong with the soles of my shoes. But when he took a breath and the color in his face subsided, I heard the word "Jesus." Now that was a first! Something about Jesus dying on a cross seemed to register in my mind. I did not know what a cross was, but this Jesus died on one. I left that morning trying to figure out some the words I heard.

That afternoon I found out we were going back that night for another round. I remember thinking, "I hope that guy who was yelling got a nap and would be in a better mood." The small crowd from the morning was even smaller that night. Here came the guy from the morning. He had on the same suit, but a different tie. He got fired up again and was talking about things we could *not* do. He did not like smoking, movies, dancing, TV, drinking, mixed swimming, shorts or Catholics. I thought that I did not care much for the Catholics either as the lady in the black outfit had chewed me out. The biggest thing I took home that night was that I was glad my mother poured out the alcohol or she would have been ticked off. It did not take much to tick her off in those days.

This trip to the south side of town was repeated again on Wednesday night. I was thinking it was really weird, but my mother had not gotten drunk, yelled or screamed at me since Sunday. So I figured whatever was going on was worth another trip because she was acting differently. The crowd was even smaller than Sunday night. I thought, "No wonder, people are picking up on his bad mood." My mother said that Wednesday night was prayer meeting night. What I did not realize then that I fully understand now is that when you call something a prayer meeting, don't plan on many showing up. One thing I have learned over the years is that prayer meetings were not attractive then, and they are not attractive now for most people.

I observed a few things that night. We only sang one song and the guy in a suit led it this time. Maybe the other guy got tired of the yelling on Sunday. The guy in the suit seemed to be in a better mood and he did not stand behind the big wooden box. He was on the floor at the front with a small stand. I thought maybe he should be down there on Sundays, rather than up on the stage behind the wooden box. My take home that night from his talk was something about a book called John and some guy who was a Baptist, lived in the wilderness and ate funny food. Then, he stopped talking and asked, "Do we have any prayer requests?"

I learned that this was not a healthy place. There were a lot of sick people. After a lot of requests he said, "Let's pray." He asked Brother Bob to open the prayer time. Then two new things I heard as a few people, and I do mean a few people, prayed. I heard a lot of "bless" so and so and "be with" so and so. I had no idea what bless meant, but I did conclude those who were sick did not have God with them because they kept asking God to be with them. Prayer was something new to me, so I tried to listen to what they were saying as

I figured this was some type of code or practice. I needed to get it down if Mom was going to keep dragging me back every week. For all I knew, the man in the suit might call on "Brother Dennis" some day, and I had no idea what I would say.

Sunday morning, Sunday night, and Wednesday night became the pattern of our week. Mom did not give me a choice or would she ever think of missing. My mom never did anything with partial commitment. She was more than a type A. She was an extremist in everything she did from drinking, to work, and now to church.

A few weeks into this new life of Mom's, I was putting some things together. Mom was changed. I asked her what it was all about. She attempted to explain in "new born" words what had taken place. I was starting to want what she had. She used terms like "Jesus came into my heart and I got saved." I was thinking that was the guy who died on the cross. So I asked about the cross deal and why He died like that. She did her best to explain sin and forgiveness. I had no theological understanding of that, but I did understand sin. I knew I had that problem. I did not have to be convinced. My teachers, principals and a few police officers could testify to that.

It was about a month into this church thing that I decided I wanted to get what Mom had. So the next Sunday before the service began, I determined I would get it. The custom of that church was that after the preacher wore himself out yelling, we would all stand and sing a song over and over, and he would ask people to come to the front. The best I could figure was that it was time that I needed to get this saved thing. I really could not explain the gospel or salvation that day, but I fully wanted to start following Jesus. So down to the front I walked on my own. I wanted a changed life. I was actually tired of being in trouble and tired of being the kid always causing problems. If Jesus helped my mom, I figured He could help me too.

I have questioned many times whether that was the day I really "got saved." I went through some periods of doubt during my first year in Bible College as I heard glorious testimonies of students who understood the full picture of the gospel the day they got saved. I thought, "Man, I did not know all of that on that day in March 1959. I have come to fully believe I responded to Jesus' words when He said, "All you who are weary, come to me and I will not cast you out." I did just that in that little church that morning. I came weary to Jesus knowing fully that I was a sinner in need of a Savior. So I have put aside doubt over the years.

I have come to realize that salvation is more than a sinner's prayer and having all the check marks lined up before that prayer. I realize that trusting in the wonderful God who provided the drawing of the Holy Spirit and gift of faith to me was truly the gift of salvation. I fully understand that only by grace and through faith does He give salvation. I am saved! Doubt has never returned.

I could write pages about my first church relating to legalism, extreme fundamentalism and separatist positions, but I won't. Though I have moved away from that camp, I still have great regard for that church and for the intensity and full commitment I learned. It was my beginning. I am eternally grateful for that pastor who yelled a lot and for strict rules that had no biblical support. That little church on the south side of town was God's choice to rescue my mother and me from total destruction.

Going back to my roots of faith brings me to a soft heart for others who proclaim the gospel whether they do so in my style or my camp. It reminds me that the power of change is in the gospel, not in the glorious way I present it.

It is the gospel that keeps us in the race, not our schemes or new and improved methods. When I remember this, I realize whether I am cool, young, or hip,

I can still proclaim this powerful gospel to my last stride at the finish line.

Clean Up Assignment

Write a paragraph or two on your first exposure to the gospel.

Think of those who were involved in getting the gospel to you and write a prayer of thanksgiving for them.

Whether you have stayed with that camp or moved to another, reflect on God's sovereignty in your early days of following Jesus. It was not an accident. Doing this creates a humble heart to see the hand of God working in your life from the beginning of faith.

Whatever you have learned from that day forward, embrace a full commitment to your job of declaring the gospel in a clear, simple way to those God has around you.

Again the Apostle Paul's words keep me in the race:

> *I have complete confidence in the gospel; it is God's power to save all who believe, first the Jews and also the Gentiles. For the gospel reveals how God puts people right with himself: it is through faith from beginning to end. As the scripture says, "The person who is put right with God through faith shall live." Romans 1.16,17 (Good News Bible).*

Chapter Three
Sink or Swim

There is one more part to the early days of faith that would be a defining event to my future. It would be too much to sort back through my twelve years of "family life" and divorces in our household. It would not add much to what has already been said and you would get bored along the way. However, there is one more event that would compound the salvation of my mother. It was my original father. My real Dad and my Mom had been divorced for most of my early years. My contact with him over the years was lean. After my mother got saved, my father traveled to our town from where he was stationed. My mother told him of her salvation. He could tell the change in her. It was about three months into her faith. He came to church with us. He came back again for a few months. Then one day he went to the front of the church at the end of service and he, too, trusted Christ and got saved. They were new people.

I can still remember that Sunday night when my Dad professed his salvation and stood in the baptism waters of that little church. I could not believe it. The bottom line was that Mom and Dad remarried and lived the next forty plus years serving Jesus. Dad eventually became a Sunday School teacher, a church treasurer and finally a deacon. God gave me not just a new Mom, but also now a new home. I began to think that this was the best life a person could have. Why would I want to do anything else but tell people that Jesus can change them?

Over the next year that pastor took me under his wing. I spent endless hours with him at hospital calls, visitations, cleaning the church, and going to pastors' conferences. As soon as school was out, I would head to the church to find him and hang around. He was more than a guy yelling in a suit; he was my pastor. When I look back, I cannot believe that a pastor would invest that much time in a twelve year old. Over the next year, I started asking him about the pastor deal. How do you get in it? How do you know you are supposed to be a pastor? One day I told him I thought I wanted to be a pastor someday. He told me I was "called to preach." I never heard the call, but I wanted to help people. I could not picture myself up there speaking and yelling. Maybe I should not have said I wanted to be a pastor. I was only thirteen. I just wanted to serve Jesus for the rest of my life because He saved our family.

It was after a Wednesday night prayer meeting that my pastor pulled me aside and said, "This coming Saturday night I want you to preach at the youth rally." It really wasn't much of a rally. It was a handful of odd kids in our church we called the youth group. There were possibly twenty-five kids on our best night, but every Saturday night we had a youth rally. When he said he wanted me to preach, I almost fainted. Honestly, I thought I did not hear him correctly or he was just joking with me. Nope, he was dead serious.

Remember, I stuttered. I would not get up in front of the class at school over the years if my life depended on it. I would not give a book report or tell of our family vacation on the first day of school each year. Obviously, for two reasons I would not get up: I stuttered and our family had no vacations as we did not have an actual family. So when he asked me to preach, I almost died! He said, "If you want to be a pastor, then it is time to get started."

The next days were the most miserable days of my life. What would I say? I didn't think I could yell and I didn't think I could even see over that big wooden box. Of course, I would stutter and make a fool of myself. I imagined kids laughing at me. I imagined myself fainting or throwing up... a total disaster. What was he thinking? I thought he liked me. Was he mad at me? This was not what I signed up for. I just wanted to help people find Jesus.

Saturday night came. I had to get my first suit and tie. Mom was so excited. Her son was the preacher boy. The only thing I halfway knew was John 3, the story of Nicodemus. I really did not understand all the details about the "wind bloweth" and entering the second time into your mother's womb. I did not even know what a womb was. The King James Version was not very helpful. What were flesh, spirit, and water? All I knew was the part of being born again meant you got saved. I tried to practice in my bedroom those days but could not stop stuttering. Finally Saturday night came.

After a few choruses and a stupid skit put on by the 8th graders, it was my turn. I thought the tie was choking me. I thought I could not breathe. I thought I was going to die! I walked up there to the big wooden box. I was about to cry. I knew the minute I spoke I would stutter and everyone would laugh. I stood there almost with tears in my eyes and said as loud as I could, "Open your Bibles to John, chapter 3." I took a deep breath. I thought it would be my final breath. Then I said, "Tonight I want to talk about a man named Nicodemus." A few more sentences came out. Then I realized I was not stuttering. No one was laughing. I kept putting sentences together and somehow made it through about fifteen minutes. I am not sure I made any sense, but two 9th graders got saved that night. When I finally sat down on the front row, actually collapsed on the front row, I realized I did not stutter throughout the whole talk. After a few days I thought maybe I was "called to preach."

That was 53 years ago. I never have stuttered since. I majored in speech in college and actually taught speech for my student teaching at a high school my senior year in college. I don't know if it was some miraculous healing because our church did not believe in miraculous healings, but I do know it was a sink or swim experience and somehow I made it out of the pool that night.

Over the next years of high school, I found my pastor throwing me in the pool many times. By my junior year, he had me preaching at youth revivals, Vacation Bible Schools, and even tossed me in a pastors' conference. I realized now that he was training me without telling me. It was not formal, not structured, but I was learning to swim in the pool of ministry.

As I write, that pastor is well into his 80's. He is still preaching the gospel miles away from me and his wife is still winning souls. We are in different camps. He would probably think I have become a heretic because I am not preaching on dancing, drinking, smoking, Catholics and movies. Yet the investment and confidence he put in me during those days I will never forget. A few years back I preached a series, "Heroes." It was focused on people who could be heroes in our church as servants, volunteers, and investors in the lives of students, children, and discipleship groups. I could not pass up the opportunity to introduce my first pastor. I flew his wife and him out from the east coast to be in our final service of the series. I did not fully tell him what I would do that morning in our three services. I just said I wanted him to see my church and the work God is doing. At the end of the message, I spoke of my first pastor and his incredible impact on my life. I had mentioned him on other occasions over the years in my preaching.

My congregation was familiar with my early days in church through the stories I told. Finally the moment came. It took everything I had not to break down and weep. I said, "Folks, I want you to meet my hero. I want to introduce to you the pastor and wife whom God used to rescue my family from devastation. Pastor, will you stand? I am so proud for our congregation to see you." He and his wife feebly stood and a long standing ovation full of tears followed. This was my hero. He was the crowning of that series. My first pastor was John Bonds and Georgetta is his dear wife. They live in Maryland today.

I go back to those early days of my Christian journey to remind all of us who lead people and pastor churches that even twelve year olds are important. It centers me back to the gospel and power of proclaiming it even if you yell and pound. It reminds me what a pastor really is. He is not a CEO. He is not a talented speaker or a slick salesman. He is a shepherd. He has sheep that need to be cared for, fed, directed, touched and loved. He is not to be on a celebrity pedestal. He is one who never forgets the importance of individuals. In today's power machine trappings of the entertained church, he remembers his calling to sheep, not the Sunday show.

I currently pastor what is considered a large church. We are the largest church in a thirty-mile circle. We are the big show in town with the latest technology and a cool building that reminds you of a gigantic Starbucks. Often I have to go back to my hero. He and I are a lot different in our style of ministry today, but in raw form he was a shepherd, a gospel preacher, and he was my pastor. He put in me courage, confidence, vision and a future. I can't forget that as I look at a multi-million dollar church budget, strategic plans, multi-site visions, and schools for emerging leaders. I have to remember the night I had to sink or swim because my pastor knew something I did not know. He knew God's call was simple, yet powerful. I will send him a copy of this book. I hope he understands how much God did through him because he was a genuine pastor.

No matter what size church you lead or what position you have in the church, don't forget you are a pastor first when it comes to ministry. Yes, our roles today demand that we are more corporate than years ago, but God's call is still to be a shepherd. Remember what shepherds do. When I remind myself of the true call of God from scripture, it stirs in me a shout out to pastors. Be shepherds first. Do not lose that as the center of your work- no matter what size the church is. The Great Shepherd will call us to account for our shepherding, not our methods, techniques, or graphs and charts. Look for twelve year olds. Look for a sheep that has a mess on aisle 2, and do not put yourself above cleaning it up. You are a shepherd.

Clean Up Assignment

Pause right now and evaluate yourself as a shepherd.

In your inventory can you identify evidence of your shepherding?

If necessary drop some office activities that keep you at the desk and find a sheep to invest in and throw in the pool and help them learn to swim.

If you do not have a plan to help others in your flock to be shepherds, take time to teach staff to make disciples of their own.

Read the verses below and remind yourself of the charge to shepherds.

Paul's charge - Acts 20:

Pay careful attention to yourselves and to all the flock, in which the Holy Spirit has made you overseers, to care for the church of God, which he obtained with his own blood. I know that after my departure fierce wolves will come in among you, not sparing the flock; and from among your own selves will arise men speaking twisted things, to draw away the disciples after them. Therefore be alert, remembering that for three years I did not cease night or day to admonish everyone with tears.

Peter's charge – I Peter 5

So I exhort the elders among you, as a fellow elder and a witness of the sufferings of Christ, as well as a partaker in the glory that is going to be revealed: shepherd the flock of God that is among you, exercising oversight, not under compulsion, but willingly, as God would have you; not for shameful gain, but eagerly; not domineering over those in your charge, but being examples to the flock. And when the chief Shepherd appears, you will receive the unfading crown of glory.

"Pastors are managers of what God owns."
- Henry Blackabee

Chapter Four
Welcome To Full Time Ministry

When high school was over, I had to make a decision about college. Because I was still engaged in a fundamental Baptist church, I did not have a lot of choices if I wanted to be true to the faith. In fact, I only had one choice and that was a Bible College in Missouri. So that was settled. Heading from New Mexico to Missouri was my plan.

Now there is one item I have not mentioned yet, but it was the next best thing to my salvation. It was the blonde that sat behind me in geometry class my sophomore year in high school. It had to be the sovereignty of God again. She was not supposed to be in the class. It was a regular geometry class. She was in advanced classes, but she had just moved to Albuquerque from San Antonio, Texas, and all of the advanced math classes were full. It was her only non-advanced class she took in high school. Her last name was Irvin, and the class was seated in alphabetical order. Man, was God taking care of me! She was smart. I was a jock who only cared about football and church.

I could write a book just on her. She was incredibly cute and I was incredibly separated from the world. I was curious about her. As the year moved on, I heard students talk about her. Boys drooled over her and the girls talked about her being a goody two-shoes. Her standards were high, her morality was impeccable and I picked up on that. I knew she was the cream of the crop. I ventured out in the spring and invited her to go bowling because I could not go to a movie, a dance or worldly party. She accepted and that began a 50-year journey. To get to the bottom line, I asked her to marry me at

Christmastime our senior year and go to Bible College.

Why in the world she said yes and our parents said okay I will never know- outside of the fact it had to be a God-thing! God knew I needed someone way above my pay grade. He knew few women could make it in ministry and especially with a dysfunctional guy like me. We got married two weeks after graduation, packed up my car and headed to the fundamentalist capital of the world where the King James Version ruled. After two years we were not challenged academically. I was learning some basic Bible stuff, but I thought there had to be more to college than this because I was making straight A's.

A medium-sized church of about 500 to 600 people in Virginia contacted me about being the youth and music pastor. They promised I could continue school at the new George Mason University nearby. It sounded good to me so off we went.

It was to be a full-time job. I missed the part that the salary did not match the job description. Besides the music and youth, I found out I would also be the printer and pick up anything else that rolled downhill. What the heck... I was in full-time ministry and someday I would be back in college at George Mason. I was now called youth pastor so money did not matter. The first year went by and I was learning and doing the job successfully. Billie was working at Safeway and we were surviving. Then my planned parenthood failed! A baby was on the way. This was not on my schedule and my salary surely would not cover another person in our one bedroom apartment. During the last couple of months of Billie's pregnancy, she had to leave the job at Safeway. She was starting to have complications due to lifting groceries and standing on her feet all day.

The loss of her income hit hard. We were barely making it with two incomes. I finally became unspiritual and asked for a raise. That request went nowhere. The pastor said that $90 a week was plenty. I don't think he majored in accounting and finance.   We lived in the cheapest apartment we could find and it was $189 a month.   Dave Ramsey says that doesn't work on his budget plan either.   Your apartment can't be half of your gross income. Because I was told and believed we should never ask for anything because God would supply, we did not tell anyone of our situation. My request to the pastor validated that thought.

We finally got to the point that we ran out of food. The electricity company was ready to turn off the service.   Every now and then my mother would send a little care package.   There would be some home-baked cookies, a couple of bags of popcorn and other goodies. The care packages had not come in a couple of months.   I was hoping that one would come because there was nothing in the house except the bags of popcorn that had stacked up over the months.

A family in the church loaned us a bed to sleep on when we first arrived. As I looked at six bags of popcorn in the cupboard, the phone rang. The couple said they were moving out of state and wanted to come by and pick up the bed. I said, "Sure, no problem."

The next day they came for the bed. I smiled and helped them load it in their truck. I came back into our apartment and there my young pregnant wife stood. She never said a negative word. We made a pallet on the floor and tried to make humorous remarks about camping out. Being close to eight months pregnant, she was already in the uncomfortable stage and now she was sleeping on the floor at night. She never complained. We thought this was God's will for us.

The next two weeks we lived on popcorn and water. That is not an exaggeration! It was not quite a healthy diet for an eight- month pregnant woman. As much as I hated church potlucks, I was checking the church calendar for one.

None were in sight. The following days I actually prayed that someone would invite us over for dinner, but no one did. No one knew. This was our cross to bear.

We were about three weeks from the delivery date so I stopped in the hospital to give them our insurance information. I gasped when the lady checked our insurance and told me we did not have maternity benefits. In those days that benefit was not automatic. There was a box that had to be checked on the application form and the church office missed it. I drove back to the apartment in tears. Did Jehovah-Jireh go on a vacation? Popcorn, water, no bed and now there was a huge hospital bill in front of us! This pastor thing had a couple of parts I did not expect.

I remembered the famous writer, George Mueller, back in the introduction to missions' class. And I remembered the ravens feeding prophets. Maybe that kind of thing would happen for us. I really did not believe God would do anything, but at least I wasn't cursing at God.

No ravens came, a milk truck didn't turn over in front of the apartment, but Wednesday night service proved God's faithfulness. After the service a member came up to me and asked if we liked fish. He had been fishing that day and had a cooler full of bass to get rid of. I would have taken sardines at that point. Another member grabbed Billie and asked if we had room for fresh vegetables in our refrigerator. She had a bumper crop in her garden and needed to get rid of a bag full while they were fresh. In the bag of fresh vegetables was a twenty-dollar bill also. We stopped by the store and picked up another bag of groceries with the twenty dollars, went home and had a feast.

This was not a great story of suffering or persecution. In fact, we look back and laugh. However, it was the first of many stories that could fill a book on God's faithfulness and trusting Him with a little discomfort in the midst of some days when we were not sure what He was doing. There were inequities going on at that time among the staff. Some things did not seem fair. We were on the brink of poverty and others were prospering with much larger salaries. I was working harder and longer than any of them. This didn't seem fair. The church was prospering, but we were going into a pit. I would not trade those days for anything. It was my first lesson in learning that real faith and real commitment never develop with ease. It comes when you have nothing to hang on to but a genuine call from God. You realize when you come through it that God was working and He was not on vacation. He always works on His time schedule.

We were in full-time ministry at full throttle. I was thinking it had to get better. As you read, your situation might make my little story look like Disneyland. I would agree with you. The clean up on this aisle is in understanding that real life ministry doesn't begin in a seminary learning languages and theories from those who have never done it but like to talk about it.

Being a pastor begins in the school of disappointment, despair and dependence. How can we preach authentic sermons to our people about life if we have been sheltered from the reality in which they live? Whether it is a shortage of money, conflict, betrayal, or sickness that is overshadowing you right now, remember, school is in session. God is always teaching us. It should start early in ministry and continue to the end. My little lesson with popcorn was not as big as I thought. God had much bigger lessons ahead!

There are many lessons we learn in our darkness. It can range from trust, pruning, and cleansing of sin in our lives, to fruits of the Spirit being developed into maturity. Whatever those periods are, most of all, they are about learning one great principle from God: He is sufficient. Paychecks, positions, equity, and recognition cannot be our security or focus. His sufficiency has to be learned. I cannot learn that by teaching or sitting in a classroom. It has to be experienced. So my best lesson on that first job that began in 1966 was to put my toe in the water of God's sufficiency. Being a slow learner, I would have to go back to school many times in the next forty plus years.

I did not plan for this book to be a theological approach to ministry or a deep Bible study. I will have to yield at this time to those who do it much better than I, but I do want to give you some verses. You have read them before I am sure. Your clean up assignment below will be to spend a good hour just reading verses that will center you back to what the Word tells us about God and our relationship with Him. Take your mind off of your elder or deacon board, your schedule, your budget, your next sermon, or your crappy situation and let His Word do its work in your heart. Put away your church growth book, your new leadership book, and your new corporate strategy plan. Just use the Bible. Just the book that we say we believe.

Clean Up Assignment

Find a quiet place.

Block everything- phone calls, texts, twitter, and email. Turn everything off.

Allow at least an hour for this clean up.

Take a pad of paper, not your computer. You will start dinking around with other things. You just need a blank pad.

As you read each verse, write a response if God says something.

- John 15:1-5
- 2 Corinthians 12:9-10
- Romans 8:26-29
- Romans 5:20-21
- Romans 8:37-39
- Matthew 19:26
- Ephesians 3:19
- Ephesians 1:22-23
- Hebrews 13:5

- I Corinthians 10:13
- Malachi 3:6
- Colossians 2:2-3
- 2 Corinthians 1:20
- 2 Corinthians 2:14
- Ephesians 3:20-21
- Psalm 1:1-3
- Philippians 4:12
- 2 Timothy 4:5
- Deuteronomy 30:20

Such is the confidence that we have through Christ toward God. 5Not that we are sufficient in ourselves to claim anything as coming from us, but our sufficiency is from God, 6who has made us competent to be ministers of a new covenant, not of the letter but of the Spirit. For the letter kills, but the Spirit gives life.
2 Corinthians 3:4-6

Chapter Five
Back To School

Attending George Mason University never came about. The ministry was too consuming. I was not academically driven, but I knew I needed a couple pieces of paper on my wall someday. A friend I met in my first college experience had taken a church in Signal Mountain, Tennessee, outside of Chattanooga. We had kept in contact over the last two years and he asked me to come to work with him and promised I could return to college. Tennessee Temple University was there and it was much more advanced than my previous Bible College. Tennessee Temple was trying to compete with Bob Jones University in the fundamental circles of academia. This was my window to stay on a church staff and continue school.

The church was small, but my friend, Jerry Prevo, was as driven as I was and was determined to build a reputable church. Knowing years were starting to slip away, I decided to get serious about school. I enrolled in twenty hours of classes and simultaneously worked about fifty hours a week at the church. I never dropped below the twenty hours a semester for the next three years and added summer sessions. Bible modules were automatically built into my studies, but that was not enough for me. I doubled my concentration load with secondary education and a speech major. I learned I could survive on two hours of sleep, coffee and a caffeine pill call NoDoz. I surprised myself and would have astounded my high school teachers as I graduated with honors. I got one of those gold seals on my diploma.

This period of my life was insane, but I was accomplishing my goals of being in ministry and continuing my academic pursuit. We had success at the church. We were the talk of the little mountain town as we grew from fifty people to over 350. We physically built a new building using men in the church, and by our measurements, did a credible job. We tried all kinds of things from bus routes, large youth rallies, revivals, concerts in public schools, and a traveling youth music group. We were cutting edge! We accomplished our goal of being the biggest church on the mountain. In our minds we were the next great church builders of the future. In reflection, it was an enjoyable experience. Jerry and I remain friends today.

Though weary over the course of that time, I was energized by chasing accomplishment and significance. I did not realize, however, that seeds were starting to germinate that were planted in my psyche back on a street corner in California. The seeds were not growing yet, just being watered. The fruit had not come forth. It would be some years before it would mature. I was unaware of the danger ahead. We are usually blind to our emptiness and lack of self-assessment, especially when we are young. I was moving up and that was all that mattered. My fundamentalist environment assured me that success was the true test of spirituality, so why would I think something was wrong.

I had much to learn about God in the future; I had no clue then. Winning souls, attracting youth, and gaining some recognition in the community were the measurements. My first of two alarms would not sound for a few more years. Remember, I am a slow learner. Evidently one alarm would not be enough.

Doing the work of God and being the work of God are two different things that a pastor must confront sooner or later in ministry. I wish I had learned it when I was younger. It is easy to be engaged in working for God and not have God working in you. Busyness is not godliness. I did not realize then that my high energy and overload were not necessarily God's first choice for me. I could not see that storm clouds were forming which would be poured out later in the midst of high points that seemed like success.

We will return to this issue later in the book. For now, let's start a few clean up checks that might save you great grief, devastation or disqualification in the future.

Clean up Assignment

Take a look at your schedule. What does it tell you?

Pray about forming a fierce accountability group for your life.

Does anyone evaluate your schedule? Or ministry? Who? When was the last time you were checked?

How does your mate evaluate your work, life, and schedule? Ask him or her.

Again, turn to Scripture. Read the passages below.

- 1 Timothy 4:15,16
- Ecclesiastes 1:2-14
- Hebrews 3:12-14
- Mark 1.9-38

After reading Mark 1:9-38, slowly do a deep inventory of Jesus' activity. Notice all He did. Measure His activity from a human perspective- physically, mentally and emotionally. What was important about verse 35?

Chart your activity of the last month. Do you see anything that might be an alert for your soul?

Chapter Six
Building My Resume

Though I had my college degree in my hand, I still wanted to add some more letters behind my name. I figured that would come in time. Now it was time to move on to bigger and better things. Jerry and I both knew Signal Mountain was just a temporary stop on our way to the bigger things. It was a good church full of wonderful people, but we both had gained confidence that something greater was ahead. We left a few months apart. I went to California to a town in the east bay area of San Francisco. Jerry went north to Alaska where he has been ever since. He has established a large ministry in Anchorage for over forty years. I was still focusing on youth work as adults really bored me. Students were much easier to motivate and mold.

Seven high school students greeted me my first Sunday and we started from there. Over the next four years things happened as I dreamed. Our youth ministry grew quickly. We were having over 400 students show up at a summer camp that only accommodated 250. We had fifth quarter pizza blasts with over 1,500 students going wild.

Before I knew it, I was being asked to speak up and down the state of California. A Bible college in southern California asked me to teach youth classes. I flew down every Sunday night to teach on Mondays and Tuesdays. Requests to hold youth ministry seminars were coming in. I was speaking at youth events and summer camps throughout the west coast. I was becoming known as "Mr. Youth" in our circles. My resume was being built and I knew this was what I was supposed to be. Some very large churches were calling me to join their staff. Things could not be better. Through all of this, my name got to a mega church; in fact, it was not only a megachurch. According to the statistics, it was about the largest church in the nation and had the largest television broadcast at that time. I believe I was sincere in all that was going on, but I did not know that my resume was going to vault me into a place that would be the first of two wake-up calls in my life.

Clean up Assignment

There is no assignment for this chapter. It will come as we move into the next chapters.

Chapter Seven
Two Alarm Calls

This is going to be a long chapter. You might get a pot of coffee or split it into a couple of readings. I know it is going to be difficult to write as I go deep into my soul and try to bring two similar stories together that were separated by eleven years and 3,000 miles. This is going to be a writing challenge as I attempt to break up the chronology of my journey. Let's see what happens.

What appeared to be success in California took me to a mega ministry. I knew this was the place to be. It was the biggest of everything. I was too intoxicated with what I thought was ministry to realize I was about to get in over my head. When you are not even thirty years old, you do not realize your limitations. Add to that an environment of pragmatism, the vision of carrying out the great commission and capturing the world, and a lot of things can go wrong.

It was 1975. I moved my family of four children and a precious ministry-oriented wife across the nation. The megachurch was fast moving with a television program and new college driving the engines. My assignment was teaching in the college and jumping into a youth ministry that was going strong but needed a lot of structure added to it. I was handed a large staff to manage and some 250-college students to train and engage in ministry. I was starting to doubt whether I could do this assignment. It was big! The total ministry of television, college and church were moving so fast that there was not a real standard of operation established.

Every gifted leader was more or less without much accountability or guidance. The silent code was "just get the job done at any cost." I did not look up the word at that time, but surely learned to live it out along with the other talented staff. The word was "pragmatism". Dictionaries give a few different definitions, but my definition is "the ends justify the means." The end was to win the world to Christ. That is a worthy end; however, I would conclude at the end of four years that the "means" or the process is important. What happens on the way to the end goal was critically important.

My first year of teaching youth courses, rewriting the syllabus for each course, working on the ten year accreditation plan for the youth major, working with the staff and college students, and speaking a few times a week in the youth department seemed to be getting done in a notable fashion. I was doing the job. The youth department was getting more structure and growing. The college students liked my classes. The college semester ended and something new came to my plate. It was decided that we needed to invade the public high schools across the southern and eastern states by doing high school assemblies with talented college students who received full scholarships. It sounded like a good idea to me. Let's find a leader for that and get it going. I did not plan on being that leader. It seemed like the natural choice for me to be the leader. Most of my focus in the church was on high school students, and I had enough music ability to take very talented singers and build a team.

The summer went orbital. Team members had to be selected, scholarships arranged, logistics planned, equipment bought and on went the list. I was not too smart, but I knew gospel music was not going to make it in a public high school assembly. I turned to a Christian musician who had worked with the best talent over the years. Disney World employed him at that time coordinating their music venues. I flew to Alabama to meet him and told him our plans. He gave me a bucketful of ideas of how to pull off a public school assembly program. It would require a whole new genre of music and had to have choreography. I knew that was going to go over like a lead balloon with an organization that did not believe in dancing. I knew we had to do it or be laughed off the stage. I hired his choreographer to train my team. We were on our way to win the public schools to Christ for that was our end goal. I knew I would take heat over this so our preparation was done in secret.

September came. We were ready. Oh, there were a couple of other things that came with this package. We would do three to four school assemblies every Thursday and Friday, local church concerts at night, and an all day youth seminar for youth pastors in the area on Saturday. Then, we would crown it with a big concert on Saturday night with students from the school assemblies and local churches. The goal was to attract hundreds of kids to a neutral site like a high school gym or auditorium. At the end of the concert, I would preach and numbers of students would get saved. The plan worked! I forgot to mention that the success brought one more item. We added an extended tour of six weeks overseas in the summer when school was out.

So let's recap how this deal went and how my schedule played out. Hang on... here we go. Monday through Wednesday mornings starting at about 7:30 AM, I would teach my full load at the college. Those afternoons I would return to the church office to meet with youth staff for planning the local church ministry. I would meet with college students who needed direction. Monday night was club night where we had Bible Clubs scattered over a thirty-mile radius with college students serving them. They needed to be supervised, so I would catch a couple of clubs every Monday and get home after 9:30 PM. Tuesday evening was my college traveling team meeting and rehearsal. Wednesday night I would speak at the mid-week youth service. As soon as it was over, I would kiss my wife and kids goodbye and jump on a college bus with my team to head to our Thursday destination for school assemblies.

An overnight eight to nine hour drive could place us anywhere from New York to Florida to Ohio and points in between. We would arrive at our destination around 6:00 AM, get showered and dressed, and start our first assembly around 8:30 AM. After the Saturday night concert I would board one of the private college planes and fly home, arriving about 4:00 AM to be ready to meet with the church youth staff at 7:00 AM. I would speak in the youth department that morning, eat at McDonald's with my family, and catch the private plane back to meet my college team halfway home for a Sunday night concert. Our bus would arrive back at the college between 3:00 AM and 5:00 AM. I would be back in the classroom at 7:30 AM and the week began again.

I hope you are still with me. Let me draw all of this together for learning. You may say, "Dennis that was insane." I fully agree *now*. However, when you are addicted to the end result, the means to get there is not inspected. When there is an internal malfunction going on to which you are numb, you ignore the process.

You might expect a toll was being taken at home. My four children did not feel the full impact because I would rotate a child every four weeks to go with me on the Thursday-Saturday trip. They loved the bus, the college students and especially the plane flight home. I would try to slip out now and then to get lunch at their schools with them. I was dropping the ball with them, but it was not as bad as the bomb I had dropped on my wife. Billie is beyond riches. She loves God more than I do and always has since I shared Christ with her in high school. She read too many books on missionaries and sacrifice during those first years of college. She accepted her lot of a widow with four children. She submitted to my schedule from hell. She entertained guests that I invited to visit us while visiting the college, and I was not even home. She stayed engaged in the youth ministry at the church. Our house was impeccable when I came home as she tried to make it as pleasant as she could for me for the few hours I was home each week. She never complained. I was blind, dumb, young, driven and an idiot. She endured it. What I did not know until years later was that most of the nights she would cry herself to sleep in loneliness.

When the pace of your life is out of control, you do not see the telephone poles as they go by. You look straight ahead at the road and nothing along the way appears important. You have a destination to reach and things that are actually important to God disappear.

There is no way possible I can actually tell you the layers of failure that were going on in the midst of pragmatic success. There were many, all of which I regret. I did prove you can do ministry and by human measurement be applauded and God have nothing to do with it.

I know you want this plane to land about now, so let me head to the runway. After two years of this schedule, I was starting to figure out something was not right. I am slow, but not a total imbecile. I asked to be relieved of the traveling team for the next year and promised I would pour that time into the local work. I am not sure everyone in the system was happy with that, but permission was granted. My fourth year at the college was starting. I added writing to my schedule. We needed to produce some youth curriculum for churches. Christmas break came. I had a couple of weeks off from the college. For the first time in three years, I had some down time. I did not do a thorough job, but I took an inventory. It was an outside inventory of my schedule, questionable practices, and family.

This surface inventory sounded my first alarm. I truly understood my ministry had grown bigger and bigger, but my heart had grown smaller and smaller. For the first time in three and half years, I knew I was messed up. I could not figure it out, but it was evident I had been living a life that was not pleasing to God, even if others applauded my work.

When January came, I knew there was only one way out of the mess I created. It had to be my resignation. It was fairly well understood if you were a stellar performer, you couldn't back down. That is why you got hired in the first place. So I sensed my value was dropping. I found myself getting bitter at my surroundings and starting to be critical. It was time to leave. I gave my resignation. I was contracted to finish the semester at the college so I had some time to get ready to exit.

I land on the runway now with a quote from Henry Blackaby's book, *The Power of the Call,* which I strongly recommend all to read. He said, "Life does not cause the condition of the heart; life reveals the condition of the heart." I want to go on record that I do not blame the mega ministry for my mess on aisle 2. I still am impressed with the work of that ministry. I understand now how things were developing there at lightening speed. I realize the inherent weaknesses of large ministries in their early stages. The problem was I was ripe for pragmatism. I do know that the first alarm went off. I did some cosmetic work on the outside, but it would take the second alarm for real work to be done in me.

Clean Up Assignment

No assignment yet. It is coming. I need the second alarm to put it together. I have given you a lot of story. I hope I did not lose you. I am really hoping it comes together after the second alarm.

Chapter Eight
Two Alarm Calls
(Continued)

I left the megachurch and went to Dallas, Texas. After a year of two senior pastors resigning, I moved from the youth pastor to the senior pastor. I remained in Dallas for eleven years. We will go back there for a brief visit in a few chapters. So stay with me; we are getting to important stuff.

It was eleven years later and three thousand miles from the megachurch when I accepted a call to a church in the San Joaquin Valley of California. The church had gone through a recent decline to about

300 people due to the moral breakdown of staff members under a loving pastor who ended up paying the price for their sins. People had been praying for a year for healing and a new pastor. When I arrived on the scene, the church was in pretty fair shape. There was not a lot of clean up to do. I would need to earn some coins of trust to be put in the bank of my leadership. I was excited. This was going to be my first real chance to prove I was a senior pastor as I had lived in the shadows of the previous regime in Dallas.

I was learning on the job for most of the eleven years there without a mentor, but now it was different. I was at, what I thought to be, the prime of my life. I was 43. (Now I think 66 or so is the prime of my life. Things are changing, you know.) I came onto the field with my normal abandonment to conquer the world, but there was a big difference from the previous megachurch experience. I was far more focused on my wife and children. The years in Dallas seemed to heal some deep wounds in Billie. She had been able to tell me of her great loneliness and hurt while there. We were processing and moving forward. Overall, the time in Dallas was pleasant and we still have fond memories and friends from the church.

I will try to give you the Cliff Notes that led to my second alarm. The church grew quickly, thanks to the long prayer gatherings that took place prior to my coming. Trust was soon established and we were on our way. About a year into our work, it was necessary to have five identical Sunday services in the small 250-seat auditorium. We were remote parking and stuffing people in. We only had five acres so we knew we had to relocate. At the end of the second year, we decided to pull the trigger. We put the building up for sale and began plans to build on twenty acres the church acquired. We calculated we would have a year or more to sell the building; after all, church buildings are hard to sell. The sale sign went up and a week later, out of nowhere, a Hispanic church gave us a contract with a 30-day move out clause. We took it.

Now what? We had no place to meet. Fortunately, after scrambling and begging, we were able to use the local high school gym, the cafeteria for student ministries, and classrooms for children and nurseries. We bought 700 padded chairs to facilitate two services that could be used later in our new building. We had to purchase platforms, tarps for the gym floor; rolls of carpets for toddlers' classrooms, cribs, and every other item needed to function. It took two eighteen wheelers to bring it in every Sunday morning at 6:00 AM and about 40 to 50 men to unload and set up the church. Of course, thirty minutes after the service, it all went back in the trucks. We rented an office building for the staff and rooms for mid-week training. It was kind of fun at first. People were actually excited, because we had hope of a new twenty-acre home in the near future.

Let me try to condense the building program from hell. Remember we are in California. (Thank You, God, that I live in

Texas now.)   It seemed simple on paper. Get an architect, a builder and get this done in a year or so. The building would be large, but simple to build. New city codes, environmental laws, endangered beetles, new city sewage, broadening the street at our expense because of increased traffic flow, sidewalks, curbs, massive underground drainage and utilities and a flakey architect started the first challenges of the project.   After $160,000 down the drain with a "Christian" architect, we were forced to find another one and a builder.

I could write about five chapters on the incredible pain of my first building program.   I now understand the statistic that 75% of pastors usually leave after the building is built.   And there was the money issue.   This was at best a middle class church.   There were no deep pockets. Every extra dollar would have to be an extreme sacrifice. It was 1992 and 4.6 million dollars was a lot of money in a small valley town. This project took twice as long as we planned.   I have led three building programs since then and this one came from the pit of hell.

While daily battles were going on with the city and delays and money trying to be raised, we still had a church to keep motivated and growing. Everyone was making financial sacrifices. Billie and I went way beyond reality in our commitment. We sold my prized Harley Davidson, cashed in our retirement, pulled savings, cut back everywhere we could, and sold cars and got old junkers, Billie went back to work full time, and we gave her income to the building fund. I had to lead by example.

During these months there were challenges coming from home. One of my children who had been married less than two years left a spouse and a child and got a divorce. In a small town that was headline gossip. Our twin daughters were leaving for college, which we could not afford because savings went to the building. My son, who was my best buddy, was growing up in high school and pulling emotionally away from me as a young man seeking his own identity. Thank God, he always lived for Jesus! He was just growing up. The problem was his father was not handling it well. Aging parents and many others things were lining up in our lives.

The ministry part was accelerating to an unmanageable level, and we could not face a decline at this point. Billie was working full time, leading four ladies discipleship groups, and involved in two large ladies' gatherings in the church. I was matching her with men's groups, staff oversight, deacons, building meetings, preaching and fighting with the city every week. Oh! I need to add one more thing. Remember, I wanted to add some more wallpaper to my name. Over the years I had been doing that. Finally, I got a Master of Theology degree. Guess what? I was working on my Doctor of Ministry degree at this time also. Just one more thing on my plate!

The old patterns of short nights and 18-hour days were coming back in my life. This time it seemed like it was survival. I had taken this church into the wilderness like Moses, and I had no idea how we were going to get back. There was no cloud in the day or fire at night. The school had lost its novelty; people were getting tired of it and a building with no completion date.

My speed was at the same pace of the megachurch days. Fortunately, three of our four kids were out of the house. Billie was there. I worked hard to stay connected with Denny, my son. He was my only breath of fresh air. He and I met every Friday morning at 5:30 AM at Carl's Jr. for breakfast over a four-year study of I and II Timothy. I pushed never to miss his soccer games and occasionally worked in a hunting trip. We were okay even though he was no longer dependent on me.

Truthfully, I felt like a drowning man with no life preserver in sight. I could not stop treading water or everything would sink. I am sure Billie was having flashbacks of the megachurch. She was hurting with daughters gone, a grandchild with a single parent, back to no money again and a husband who was going deeper into his cave of non-communication. Add to all of that, she was going through menopause which I had no clue of how that impacts a woman. The second alarm was about to go off.

When the alarm sounded through the most serious request from Billie to have a talk, I was devastated. I don't need this now. I have to keep this church going. I can't stop! I did not know how to handle the alarm. The sound was defeating. I have failed as a husband. Guilt flooded into my soul. Now it all started sinking in! I was a failure at what was very precious to me- my role of a husband. I always treated her with kindness. Let me pause to tell you that in forty-eight years of marriage, we have never argued, yelled or had any confrontational meetings. My children will testify to that. I deserved to be yelled at over the years, but she was an incredible wife.

You would think that I would respond and fix this thing. With full awareness this time that I had allowed the monster to return in my life, it put me in a deeper cave. It took every ounce of fortitude I had to get from Sunday to Sunday. I was thinking I should just quit and go back to a grocery store. I probably never should have been a pastor in the first place. I really was nothing but a kid from a dysfunctional upbringing that should have just stayed in the meat department or checkout stand. The reality of my ineptness had been exposed.

So what does a pastor do at this point? What were my options? I knew I needed some help, counsel, or friend. Counseling was out of the picture. We did not have $150 per hour for that. Furthermore, I was probably too proud to seek one. I figured counselors were crazier than I, or they would not be in the business. Should I talk to my deacon board? No way... I have heard of the disasters of boards turning on a pastor. I did not have any friends I could trust or a wise mentor in my life. My staff was all younger than I, and I could not let them know I was about to drown. They needed a stable leader. So what did we do? After my initial despair, we slowly started working back. I began to look deep in my soul to try to discover what was wrong with me. In the next chapter I will share what I learned. The good news is we came out of it. I have since discovered many pastors don't. The statistics I have found from a variety of sources report around 1,600 pastors in the United States leave the ministry each month.

Clean Up Assignment

This assignment is not detailed. Based on the mess you have just been reading, is anything resonating with you? Are there any connections to my personal mess on aisle 2? Be critically introspective. Ignoring a twinge that might have come while reading this will not help you. Be brutally honest with yourself. Are there any spills going on in your life to which you need to pay attention? I suggest some serious inquiries with the Holy Spirit right now and some extended listening.

Chapter Nine
My Aisle 2 Clean Up

I was in a cave and coming out when I had an available moment to continue a running series of conversations with Billie. I was trying to deal with our situation of ministry, family, and our relationship as a couple that dearly loved each other and both seemingly never needing much maintenance. She was a trooper and I unintentionally took advantage of that. On the outside she was the sweetest, kindest person anyone would meet. She was the ideal pastor's wife who was a merciful, compliant model of Christ. What many did not know was that she was the strongest, toughest person there could be as she had put up with me for twenty years. Again, we had no hints in our home or public life of mistreatment. We got along very well and I truly adored her. However, the second alarm from her this time revealed that I had actually been abusive by my priorities of life being totally screwed up. She knew I never meant to be. I could not put my finger on it until her "Popeye" moment as the old saying goes, "I stands all I can stands, and I can't stands no more." The insanity had to stop!

We are now on my aisle 2. I can't step around the mess this time. I can't cosmetically fix it by changing locations. I had enough character and resolve to know I had to finish the building and hold this growing congregation together. My aisle 2 had to be fixed this time. I had to figure out why I dropped the jars. I have already told you I am not the brightest bulb in the package. I had enough experience in counseling people, psychology courses, and seminars to have some information with which to work. I set aside my doctorate work. I used extra hours to be quiet, pray, and go into the Word. I asked the Holy Spirit to show up and really do His promised work of being my Counselor, my Paraclete… my true teacher. I understood how empty I really was.

Some of you may have already been thinking, "Dennis, let me give you some answers." It is obvious to you that words like self-identity, performance driven, self-acceptance, self-esteem, self-dependence, misguided priorities, and impure motives might apply. You are in the right neighborhood. I had taught lessons on all of those topics over the years. Now, I was looking long in the microscope to my soul. The lessons I had taught were coming more clearly. Yes, they were the minimal realities of my life. Let me also throw in subtle pride in case you overlooked it. Acknowledgment and confession of those issues were coming forth now with true tears of repentance. Conversations with Billie in identifying those things were helping. She was an amazing listener. She would speak at the right time with words far wiser than I could conjure.

As those issues were being addressed in my journal, prayers and conversations, I knew the clean up was not done. The floor was still sticky. What was causing all of that? With my fundamentalist upbringing I could narrow it down to a couple of words- sin and sin nature. I knew that, but it felt like an escape or excuse. I needed to get to one more level and then try to work backwards to put it all together.

I had no visions or voices or miraculous revelations. Yet, over the course of the next months, I believe it was the Holy Spirit, not a psychiatrist, who took me back to a street corner in California. I realized seeds were planted there. Some of you can remember that era. It was the Wally and Beaver days, and Ozzie and Harriet. Divorce was not acceptable or the norm. I was always the odd kid in class. "Tell the class what your family did over the Christmas holidays," the teachers would ask. Everyone gave a joyful story. Me? We had drunken fights, yelling and screaming. No it wasn't my mom and dad. It was a stepfather or boyfriend. We even shared Christmas with the cops as they showed up for the domestic disturbance call. I don't need to go into more details of early childhood; you've been getting the picture.

I realized that on the street corner throwing newspapers began my journey of self-worth. I could out work anyone. It was my security, my identity. It was the way I could be recognized by Mom. She was proud of me when I worked. It was the only way I could feel good inside. What I hated at 5:15 in the morning actually became my closest companion for the next forty years. I was up before anyone else. I earned money that other first graders could not think of earning.

My closest companion unknowingly had moved into my soul to be my very best friend. He went with me into the grocery store, the football field, the college classroom, the racquetball court, a police car, and friendships. Worst of all, he went into ministry with me. He would whisper in my ear in the middle of the night, "You need to get up. You have to prove to everyone you are valuable. You can't let them know you are a scared kid on the street corner who knows he is not worthy to be in ministry. You've got to get going." Billie could tell you of the nights early in our marriage when I would sit up in bed from a deep sleep and she would ask, "What's wrong?"

I would ask in a daze, "What am I supposed to be doing? Where am I supposed to be?"

She would answer, "It's two o'clock in the morning. Go back to sleep."

My "close companion" would draw even closer and speak louder when overwhelming challenges came of which I was incapable. He would help me accomplish the extreme in every case. What I thought to be a friend was actually my damning enemy- the deceiver of my soul. When your work is in eternal matters of the great commission, pastoring, working for God, blindness to your enemy can easily set in. I love God; I am in His work. Denying myself and bearing my cross all excused "my friend". I had more Bible verses than I needed to justify my lifestyle. Paul worked and labored to exhaustion in Thessalonica. I was convinced I was only following a biblical model.

I came to realize it was more than a good work ethic that lived in my soul. Everything was a challenge. There was always something to prove and some identity to be established. Everything I did could quickly turn to competition and I could not lose. The biggest youth group, the biggest church in town, or the fullest calendar all watered the seeds from the corner. Now at age forty-six, the harvest had come. The fruit was bitter- hurtful to my soul, to my wife, and my relationship with the God who had already accepted me.

By now you have already started tying the ends up of my psyche. It is evident to you, isn't it? It is harder to detect when covered with legalism, pragmatism, visions of ministry, a high calling and helping the lost. When you can teach great truths from Scripture on these issues and are applauded, it is easy to miss your own absorption of the truth. Messages of truth are easy to put together after years of doing it. You teach it so you must understand it and possess it, but I didn't. My soul never got it.

There were other friends my constant companion recruited as we journeyed together. The list is too long to write about. Never saying out loud, but by my actions, I would evaluate others. I would quietly think, "Why can't you work like I do" as I told them not to follow my example. There were many broken jars on aisle 2. You detect the mess.

Even now, I believe I was sincere in my journey. I wanted God's work to flourish for His name. I was just blind to the depth of God's acceptance, grace, and my position as a son. I do believe I loved God, but in reality I loved my companion more because he was measurable, visible.

I am sure you are worn out by now. So let me give you a few things I had to learn in cleaning up my aisle 2. Remember, I hated hearing, "Clean up on aisle 2." It was the unpleasant work of the store. Through the reality of the Holy Spirit's work, I finally started to believe the truth about my position with God. I truly began to believe I was accepted. I gained much ground in my understanding of grace, adoption, full redemption, and identity in Christ. I began to learn to actually pray genuine prayers of surrender, dependence on my Father and not my companion. I started thanking God for my upbringing as a child and for a mother and father who were trophies of grace. I thanked God for my spiritual roots. I did not blame anyone or anything. I actually thanked God for megachurches and fundamentalism. They were not the problem. My shallow belief system was the problem. As in Romans 1, I exchanged the truth for a lie. I listened to my companion on the street corner. I processed through a fuller understanding of God's sovereignty. I began to leave that street corner. I moved to a throne room where my Father awaited to whisper in my soul, "You are complete, fully accepted and totally approved by me." He would often tell me I was worth more than work and accomplishment. The words I heard in 1959 from Jesus now became more powerful and real, "Come unto me all you who are weary and heavy laden." I realized I did not have to work to maintain my position of value. I was valuable because He was a worthy God who had already demonstrated my worth on a cross and a resurrection.

It was a turning day when my aisle 2 started being cleaned up in quiet moments and not public platforms of ministry. It was not instant or necessarily a panacea victory. It was acknowledged, confessed and in sight now. I would return to aisle 2 again, and unfortunately often, but I could see the mess each time. I knew where the mop bucket was and would ask the Holy Spirit to grab the mop for me. I could catch jars many times before they broke.

I suspect my story is not that intriguing or glorious for many of you who are of a much deeper faith than I. I have not written with any idea that this would be some profound new insight or truth that would begin some new movement. The story of my aisle 2 is not what I want you to remember. I have shared aisle 2 prayerfully for the purpose that God might use it to help you as you run the race of ministry. I feel deeply for pastors, leaders, and believers who are sincerely trying to run with all diligence. I know how many hazards there can be on the track of a pastor. I sincerely pray that possibly this will help you be aware of your aisle 2 as you journey. Yours can be totally different than mine. Your jars may look different. I just pray that you can avoid some of the jars I dropped.

Clean Up Assignment

This is the most ambitious assignment I have given. I originally planned to give you a lot of passages from scripture. They are beside me on my yellow pad. Then I realized aisle 2 clean ups are personal. I had to dig through months of clean up for Scriptures. I want you to do the same. It is not an easy assignment. Aisle 2 was always unpleasant when I walked over there. The same is true in spiritual clean up. I look back and realize I had to come to desperation before I began. I do not want to make it easy on you. If you are not desperate, then a quick and easy fix will not help.

In the grocery business, our regular inventories told us our standing. Go back to Chapter 9 and connect with what you did there. You are now approaching deep inventory time. It won't be done between chapters of this book. It will come in layers.

The Holy Spirit is now in control. You can't rush Him. He is the boss; you are not. Don't force or short change this process. Just get started.

If your inventory is revealing your dropped jars, now start digging for Scriptures. The Paraclete will come along as promised and reveal all things to you.

Confession, repentance and restitution are next on this assignment. Besides your wonderful God, with whom do you need to talk? With whom do you need to make restoration and request forgiveness? Let the Holy Spirit guide you as you *slowly* make your list. Of course, this has to be prayer directed.

No matter how terrible your circumstances or surroundings, do not place the blame there. Take responsibility for your response to the circumstance, not what the circumstances drew from what was in you. Remember Blackaby's statement in Chapter 7.

Begin to thank God for what is on your inventory. Romans 8:28 is always a well-used verse, but it cannot be read without verse 29. Verse 29 is the **purpose** behind everything. Many times it takes aisle 2 to understand verse 29. I probably would not have started my growth to verse 29 without my aisle 2.

> *And we know that for those who love God all things work together for good, for those who are called according to **his purpose**. For those whom he foreknew he also predestined **to be conformed** to the image of his Son, in order that he might be the firstborn among many brothers.*

Chapter Ten
In The Front Seat This Time

In the process of leaving the megachurch, I wondered where I would go from this platform. Did I really want to go to just another church? Did I want to work with a pastor who I would overpower? Maybe I needed a break from ministry for a while. In my search for a job, I ran across a motivational company in Waco, Texas. After two trips for interviews, they were ready to hire me for my potential speaking ability and my experience with youth. They liked my potential to write motivational courses for youth. The contract was incredible. It was more money than I ever thought I would make. After weeks of prayer I decided I could not do it. I was called to God's church and couldn't forsake that call. A pastor in Dallas whom I met ten years earlier had followed my career. We crossed paths at DFW airport on a return home. He told me I would have the freedom I wanted if I would work for him. They were small then, but had great potential in youth ministry. I trusted him, so I accepted his offer.

The next eleven years I would be in Dallas. I had no idea what was ahead. Three months into my taking the job, he resigned. Within the next months the next senior pastor resigned. This was great. I had been there just a year and two pastors had resigned. One left as a result of marriage difficulties, and the other due to health issues. Unknown to me, I learned there was a colorful history of staff failures (I have since learned to do better research on a church before I get too far in the hiring process).

The deacons asked me to preach for a while to let the dust settle. Three months later I was the senior pastor with 98% vote. I never figured out who the 2% were. Whoever they were, they never caused a problem. I never thought I would be a senior pastor. Actually, I took the position with some reluctance, but figured it was time to be in some control of my destiny. The next ten years were a learning experience. I really had no idea what a senior pastor did. Thankfully, the people were patient and loving and let me stumble along. Because of God's humor and grace, we did move forward and I began to have a pastor's heart.

When I was six, I never dreamed I would end up in the front seat of a police car. One Friday night after two years of being in Dallas, I was sitting in the front seat of a Dallas police car as a civilian observer at 11:30 PM. I did not know this would be the ride of my life. A deacon who had become a good friend was a Dallas police officer. He did not know I had been praying about ministry outside of the four walls of my office. I missed life with students on the campus, somewhat in

the real world.   I was becoming too
clerical.   I prayed for God to open up
something where I could be with sinners.
He did!   That ride led to many other
Friday nights.   I was a pastor, so I could
ride whenever I wanted.   By now you
sense my personality.   Risk, action, and
pursuit resonated with me.

When each Friday night came, I was
ready.   What became clear to me were the
needs of police officers.   They had their
own world. We call it the "blue circle."   It
is difficult to penetrate.   After months of
riding, the first watch lieutenant pulled me
aside and said, "You are out here a lot and
it is dangerous. The officers like you. Have
you thought about joining the
department?"

"I would love to, but you know I
pastor a church and that is my first
calling," I replied. He told me about the
reserve program. The Dallas Police
Department probably has the best reserve
program in the nation.   The training was
like the regular officers, just longer because

classes were at night. When graduation was completed, reserves were empowered and commissioned like a regular officer. Reserves had to fulfill a minimum number of hours each month, but they could choose their schedules.

The next Monday I was at police headquarters starting the entire process for application. It was not a given I would be chosen. There were only one hundred reserves officers with over 2,200 regular officers. Lengthy background checks, psychological testing and interviews, a polygraph test, and intellectual tests were all part of the hiring routine. It was a three-month process. If I passed all of that, then the final step was the ominous police review board. It was notorious for trying to break down the applicants. Passing all the other requirements would be out the window if I failed the police board. I was the only interviewee that day. I walked into a small room with ten seasoned police officers sitting around the conference table. No smiles, no welcome, no greetings were offered when I walked in. I stood there waiting.   A vice officer did not even look up but gruffly said, "Sit your ass down."

I thought, "Hey, I am applying to be one of you. Did I walk in the wrong room?" I wanted to move up to the front seat this time. It seemed like thirty minutes of silence followed. Copies of my file were being looked through. I was sweating now. Finally an old donut-eating veteran grunted and said, "Well," in about four syllables. I looked over at him. He stared at me coldly. I was told not to show any sign of weakness or intimidation. I was not going to back off, so I stared back as mean as I could.

With his elongated stare and the silence, I calculated we had been in there an hour. I was not going to break the stare and look at my watch.   I was trying to convince myself by saying in my brain, "Bring it on, Fatso."

Finally, he started again. "Well, what in the hell is a f------ pastor doing in here? Why don't you get up and go baptize some baby?" I wanted to tell him Baptists did not baptize babies. "This is not some pansy, feel good job. This is a war zone. You're not applying to be a Boy Scout leader. I can't believe you had the stupidity to even walk in here." I dared not look around the table. I did not want to appear I was looking for help. I was determined I was going to keep staring back at Mr. Donut. I waited for his next statement. "I don't see any record of your being in the military." He paused.

I thought I had better spit out something. "I applied for Vietnam, but I got a 4F classification because of an ACL surgery my senior year due to a football injury."

Another officer pitched in, "Did you trip on the water bucket?"

"No, Sir, I replied, "a 285 pound tackle and a linebacker scissored my right knee after running 143 yards in the first half." Things got quiet for a moment. I think that took them off guard.

Thirty-five minutes of rapid fire questions followed with police scenarios where I had to decide on the spot without hesitation how I would respond. Questions about "Thou shall not kill" and if I would take someone's life had to be answered. I had already answered that on the polygraph test, but they needed to drill me on it. Finally, with the same tone I entered the room, they told me to leave and sit outside. Ten minutes later a uniformed captain came out and said, "Preacher, welcome to the Dallas Police Department... if you make it through the academy."

I have to compress eight years of police involvement. Cops are great storytellers so I will try to give you the quick history and purpose of this chapter. My police work, as most things in my life, went to the extreme. My motive was real ministry of helping cops in a real world. I graduated as president of my academy class and gave the graduation speech. The night I graduated, I headed straight to

Northwest Station where I was assigned to ride my first shift on what was called, "first watch"- 11:30 PM to 7:30 AM. I went back to the academy later on to earn my full police officer status. I honestly believe this was a God-directed journey. I established myself as an outstanding officer in my work. God gave me the opportunity to do a number of funerals of police officers lost in the line of duty. As you might know, those are big events with hundreds of officers and full news coverage. Of course, I doubled and tripled the minimum hour requirements each month.

I was learning things I never learned in college or seminary. I was learning how to be among the lost without fear. Lost people were real people. I was out of my office mixing with sinners. Some prostitutes I arrested eventually came to my church and ate in our home. That was probably not a smart idea as an officer. It was a fine line of policy violation. In all my years with officers, I never invited a cop to church. I established my presence with them as a partner and not a preacher.

They would initiate the God conversations. They would ask for help with their marriages, kids, and police pressures. They came to church on their own by the numbers. I married them, played ball with them, and went hunting with them and on vacations. God had answered my prayer to be among the lost.

About mid-way in my career, the chief of police asked me to lunch. I had only shaken his hand at funerals and on the day of my graduation. Was I in trouble for the prostitute deal? Small talk began. I learned about his life and I shared a little of mine. Finally, he slowly thanked me for my contribution to the department. He said, "You have had a great impact. What else do you want to do in the department? I know you are not out here because you like staying up all night." After some discussion he decided I needed to teach in the police academy. Wow, this was a God-appointment! I would be in front of every recruit. One of my mottos was "Take this job and shove it or take this call and love it." In a three-hour session I finally would land on Romans 13, where God says to submit to the authorities. By the way, the police chief started attending my church and eventually trusted Christ.

I would love to tell you police stories at this point. In my story files are high-speed chases, bar fights, and burglaries in process. My partner and I were in a shooting my first months on the streets. A lady shot a man, and I wrestled the guy to the ground. Glad he had a bullet in his stomach, because he was huge. I have been with officers as they died on the streets. On go the stories. Cops being my best friends, getting saved and baptized are my greatest memories.

On the career side, I was awarded the "Commendation Bar" for outstanding service at the annual awards banquet. Only a handful of officers ever get this award, and it was unheard of for a reserve officer to get it. Most of all, it was a God-anointed venture. My witness became my life, not my pulpit. My view of the lost changed; my preaching changed. My prayer to be out of the four walls was answered. I thank God for a dimension of ministry that I could have never experienced in a church building. I felt a little more like Jesus eating with sinners.

You may be wondering, "Okay, Dennis, why in the world did you take paper and ink for this story?" I felt I needed to share it because many pastors and church leaders do not understand the non-believing world. As pastors, we are chained many times to our offices, church buildings, and Christian activities and lose touch with the world Jesus lived in- eating with sinners.

We preach the great commission, but many times I have found myself not really engaged in it. I write to remind myself to walk out of the building, find a place among the lost and live as Jesus did. When I renew those activities, everything changes. The stakes of the gospel are higher. The urgency of my calling returns. Pastors have to remember that shepherds go after lost sheep, not just groomed sheep with Sunday School ribbons. When pastors make the famous statement, "Jesus is the answer," I wonder if they even know the questions the lost are asking. If pastors, amidst everything else they do, will get dirty with the lost sheep, they will run the race with a much different stride.

I loved the front seat of a police car. I am thankful that I never returned to the back seat. The front seat gave me a true view of the world.

Clean Up Assignment

This is your evangelism clean up. This is a moment of truth.

When was the last time as a pastor you actually hung with sinners? Discount your visitation program. I mean when have you sat and had a beer with the lost (a Coke for the Baptist)?

Don't excuse yourself because you are a pastor who has to study, visit the sick, attend meetings, etc. Today's assignment is to pray as I did in 1981, "Lord, direct me to a place outside of my office where I can really live among sinners as Jesus did."

As usual, I overcommitted my schedule with the DPD. You do not have to put the hours I did in the DPD. Your assignment for this clean up is to start clearing your calendar for a few hours each week of intentional penetration with love into a setting with non-believers. It could be a university, a club, or a neighborhood. Get your butt out of the holy place.

Read Luke 15 each day for a week. Trace back through the Gospels the activities of Jesus with sinners at parties, weddings and teaching. Remember, the Pharisees would stand and murmur.

Chapter Eleven
If We Don't, Who Will?

Let's pick it back up in the San
Joaquin Valley. Remember, this church
was where I went from Dallas. The
building program from the pit of hell was
completed. We were ready for our first
services. We added more chairs. We were
set up with a thousand seats. We would
have two services and all would be well.
When the doors opened, the excitement
was incredible. Both services filled up and
we were out of parking space. Yes, we
fixed the permanent facility problem
because it was much better than unpacking
two 18-wheelers at 6:00 AM. I enjoyed the
next two years in that building and the

church continued to grow. It was now an enjoyable place.

I was mid-way in my seventh year when a church in the "other" valley called. It was one of the most historic churches in California, approaching 150 years. It was in the Silicon Valley. The area enticed me. This was the Mecca of every high tech company- Apple, IBM, Siemens and Cisco; however, the church had no appeal for me. I was familiar with the church. My brother had been a pastor a few miles away in Los Gatos. I will never forget his words of advice, "Run as far as you can away from that church. It is dead and you will die with it."

I asked a few other pastors in that area and similar comments came. One said, "It is the church no one wants to pastor." Okay, that confirmed my thinking. No way would I even consider a face-to-face interview. "The next call that comes from them, and this little venture is over," I thought. I was wrong.

The process that led me to this church took over six months of on and off discussions. There were hours of wrestling with a large number of mean-spirited deacons who hated Rock and Roll music, worship singers, and casual worship. They had no idea who Chris Tomlin, Matt Redman or Dave Crowder were. This was the historic "First Church," and it was communicated loudly. It was the antithesis of my church I was pastoring. Our church in the San Joaquin Valley was growing with the lost being saved. The congregation was young and relevant. In contrast, this church had experienced a record decline from over 3,000 attendees to about 300. They were elderly and out of touch with the culture. It was filled with traditions and practices that had disconnected them from what was taking place around them.

After one long, heated interview that I knew would be the last one, Billie and I walked out to our car in the parking lot. It was after 10:00 PM. The church sat on a hill that had a million dollar view of the Silicon Valley. We sat there stunned.

"How could leaders of a church be so stubborn, mean and out of touch with the real world," I thought. I told them in my closing comments that night that the Titanic was sinking and they were shuffling deck chairs. I told them, "You need to figure out where the hole is and fix it!" As we sat there for a few minutes looking out over one of the most strategic cities in America, I broke the silence and said, "If we don't take it, who will?" There were young bucks out of seminary bondage desperate for a job that would. They would be chewed up and spit out. We cried and prayed God send a Moses to rescue them from there.

I had just finished reading a book by George Barna entitled *Turn Around Churches*. The book was his research of churches that experienced severe decline. Few made it back. The ones that did acquired a pastor with experience and somewhere around 45 years old. I was a little past the average age, but I had the needed experience now. I have never figured out to this day how I determined

God's will. It was never a voice from heaven or clarion call. It was one of those things I just sensed. Sitting there that night, I had one of those "sensing episodes." I thought, "God, you're not serious are you?" I guess He was. A few weeks later the church voted in a yelling match they entitled a church "business meeting." I was told it went on for two hours. (To God be the glory.) I needed a 75% vote. The chairman called me after the vote. He was elated. The church had called me with what he said was an outstanding vote. I asked, "How outstanding was it?" He proudly told me 75.2%. Why I accepted that call I still don't know outside of, "if we don't, who will?"

I remember my first Sunday there sitting down on the front row on a pew that had a spring that jabbed me in the rear end and looking at a choir in robes that had not changed in fifty years. As the choir sang (more or less), I thought of the great worship back in the San Joaquin church with a rockin' band and young singers. I leaned over to Billie and said, "I think I have made the biggest mistake of my life." That was a great encouragement to her.

In my previous two churches we never had mean people. I never received a hateful letter or vicious comment cards from Sunday services. I was about to be introduced to things I had heard about but never experienced. In the first two years there was never a week that we did not receive a critical comment. The church was already dead and in debt. I was just praying we could have some form of resurrection. The Silicon Valley had quickly and dramatically changed since the church moved from downtown to the "Hill" in 1970. Sadly, most of the church did not know it. They were at least thirty years behind reality. The building, which at one time was state of art, was now old and run down. It smelled like an assisted living home. There were 2600 seats in the auditorium with about 300 blue hairs sitting all over in the seats they had held for years. They would die for tradition and they were proving it. There were a handful of young couples. Many of them were raised by parents who believed Bill Gothard was part of the Trinity.

If you have been around churches and know the stories of churches that refused to change, then you will understand my situation. I removed the large pulpit the size of a bedroom and brought in a stool. You would have thought I crucified Jesus. When I stopped wearing a suit and tie for more casual attire, I might as well have worn a Speedo. Every change was from hell for many of them.

I was not a young kid out of college trying to change for change sake. I was an experienced pastor who knew that insanity was to keep doing what you have been doing and expect different results. I knew not to make sudden changes. I was trying to use the clutch when we shifted gears.
In the eight years I spent there, we did grow and we did change and life came back. We were starting to get some traction. Then the "dot com" implosion

occurred which caused the loss of over 75,000 jobs over night in the tech valley. The 9/11 crisis occurred which affected the national economy. The young couples we were starting to reach were exiting the valley. Somehow, we kept growing. It was not a stellar growth, but it was measurable and steady. Believe it or not, we built a two-story junior high building for the school connected with the church. (By the way, I still hate building programs.)

I could write many pages about the war that took place on the Hill. I could write a modern real life commentary on I Peter 3 and 4 about suffering while trying to do good. I do want you to know there were some good and visionary people among the crowd. Fortunately, their numbers began to multiply and after four years, things turned around.

I share this portion of my journey for leaders who are facing a situation that is difficult. I learned many lessons about leading a church through something needed but not wanted. Tom Landry, the legendary coach of the Dallas Cowboys, once said, "Coaching is getting men to do things they don't want to do, to gain what they want to have." So it is with churches. Change is never easy, but it is necessary and best. I learned that vision and change came, not from the inspired messages in the pulpit, but over coffee at a café with individuals sharing their hearts face to face. It came by focusing on the lostness of the culture around them and not the change itself. I sat with aged grandparents and talked about their grandchildren. I asked them why they thought they had turned away from the church. God allowed me to touch their hearts for future generations.

There were many delicate conversations where I had to depend on the Holy Spirit to open their hearts and not attack their failed past. I had to become a wordsmith of biblical truths about the harvest that was ripe and waiting. I learned to put aside my normal aggressive vision casting to bite-sized, palatable pieces. I learned that strategic plans were not what they needed to hear. They needed to sense a loving shepherd who was trying to lead them. As I look back, I realize I was learning more than they were. My whole mode of operation needed to adjust.

The greatest lesson I can share with pastors who are living with horrendous situations is that a wise and gentle shepherd is the foremost need. This does not eliminate strong determination. It means you can drive cattle, but you must lead sheep.

There is a price to be paid when your assignment is to be a change agent for the sake of God's church. Many times it is a high price, but it is always worth it when God performs a turn around. If you are in the middle of an aisle 2 situation, be patient, strong and most of all loving. Find a mentor who has been through this ahead of you. Seek their counsel. Most of them will be glad to walk with you through the minefields.

Some of my preset goals for the church were never obtained. I did, however, answer the call that I wanted to turn down. I do believe we went where no one else wanted to go and God smiled. We answered the question, "If we don't, who will?" The church remains today with continued hope for reaching the Silicon Valley.

Clean Up Assignment

Prayerfully assess your church. Identify any opposition. Write down how you have tried to deal with it in the past. What can you change in your relationship with opponents? Ask God to reveal to you how you can relate to them in a better way. Spend some serious time reading I and II Thessalonians. Write a model of how Paul ministered to that church. What did he do that you might adopt into your present situation?

Could it be that you need to take a new mode of operation with the flock you are leading? Sometimes we become part of the problem.

Pray for God to lead you to a mentor who has walked your path. Contact that person and request their help.

Search for books that deal with change. Many of them will be in the business realm.

Read and internalize Psalm 78:70-72:

> *He chose David his servant*
> *and took him from the sheep pens; from*
> *tending the sheep he brought him to be the*
> *shepherd of his people Jacob,*
> *of Israel his inheritance.*
> *And David shepherded them with integrity*
> *of heart; with skillful hands he led them*
> (New International Version).

Chapter Twelve
Just Add Water

Eight years passed for us in the Silicon Valley. Ministry had become pleasant and comfortable. I was thinking this could be a long run. Then an unusual six-week period came. I received five phone calls from churches across the country inquiring whether I would consider talking with them about being their pastor. At first, I politely stated I was content where I was and did not think I was really interested. However, five calls in a short period of time caused me to think that I might need to look into them. This might be a signal from God for a change I was not contemplating. I began a four-week investigative journey of flying from one place to another meeting with search committees. Oregon, Virginia, Dallas and Austin were my stops. All of the churches were of good size ranging from 1,000 to 2,500 in attendance. Some of them were intriguing. A couple of them were ready to offer me a call.

A fifth and final option came to the surface, a church in Sherman, Texas. It was the smallest church on the list with just over two hundred in attendance. The thought of returning to Texas did interest me, as I became a Texan in heart after living in Dallas. In the back of my mind I always thought I would end my journey in Texas. Retirement was never a real option in my mind, but ending in Texas was appealing. I began several weeks of phone conversations and conference calls with this smaller church. Finally, Billie and I flew to Texas to meet the folks face to face. It was a warm experience. Typical Texas hospitality was given to us. I missed that Texas culture after being in California for fifteen years. It felt like home. A second visit followed. Four months of interaction took place and now we were at the point of decision. I was asked at the end of the process, "What is your evaluation of our church?"

I responded, "You are the smallest church with whom I have talked; however, I believe you are the healthiest church of all of them." They asked what I thought and I said, "After thoroughly studying your history and present status, I think all you need is a coach and a playbook. You have been a solid Bible teaching church, but you have never capitalized on your church growth opportunity." The deal was sealed and in mid-November 2004, we relocated to Sherman.

I was coming to Sherman with a peace and calmness which I had learned through my aisle 2 clean ups. I did not have to prove anything. I did not have to build the biggest. I wanted to be a shepherd and lead them with one focused goal of *making disciples*. For the first time in 38 years of ministry, numbers and size did not rule me. I was not the driven pastor of my past. At the same time, let me assure you, I had not arrived by any means to the saint level. I was growing just to be the shepherd God wanted me to be. I did not desire to drop the jars of my past. Now that does not mean I had perfected my high energy or strong work ethic, but I was definitely in recovery.

I made some requests and asked for some agreements in the discussions with leaders before I moved. I stated, "I believe God will do what He wants with size and growth if we would focus on loving God passionately, *making disciples* and developing a praying church." Prior to coming to Sherman, prayer had become a non-negotiable part of our church life for me. I concluded I think we will grow, but that will be God's choice. Our choice was to walk in obedience to those goals. Full agreement came.

I asked for one more agreement that would be a deal breaker. I said we had to be for the Kingdom, not just build *our* kingdom. I said, "We need to pray, support, and build trust with other gospel preaching churches in our area." Thus, I requested we pray for a church each week in our services. In addition, I asked that we would pray for 25 to 30 churches in our new upcoming monthly prayer meetings. I also asked that I would be allowed time to engage in helping pastors in the area through encouragement, fellowship, mentoring and prayer. This resonated with them. I knew I was in the right place.

We got to work and prayerfully started to get a playbook for the church. It was not so much charts and plans, but it was more on focus. By the end of the first year things were moving forward, parking lots were getting full, and walls were being taken down for more seating space. We added more parking spaces. We were at two services and had done all we could do to accommodate the crowds. We added a third service in the morning. Then we added two more services in our largest room for a simultaneous video venue. We were able to add more seats, but that created unmanageable parking problems.

Traffic flow was bottled. We were parking down the side streets for blocks and our staff and leaders were parking at a remote sight with shuttle service.

It was apparent we would stunt our growth if something did not change. "Oh, no," I thought, "not again." Yep, it was time not only to build, but also to relocate. Our five acres would not accommodate future growth. I had been through this identical scenario before in California twelve years earlier. Fortunately, I was a little wiser. I knew I needed help. We acquired an executive pastor to manage the project. I would raise the money, keep the vision going and preach. We interviewed five good candidates. None of them seemed to be the right fit. Then Billie suggested a name to which I responded, "No way, he would not even consider it." To my surprise, he did and he came. I will tell you about him in a moment when I introduce our team of all-star coaches.

We set some financial goals to reach before we would start construction. We doubled the minimal goal and we were on our way. We purchased twenty acres of property nearby. Talk about déjà vu. It seemed like a repeat of the San Joaquin Valley in California.

We opened for our first service in late January 2009 with two morning services. After a few weeks we had crowded parking lots again. You got it; we had to pour more concrete. As I write we are in three morning services and have recently added a simultaneous video venue during a service that will temporarily accommodate an additional 250 people. We project we will have a second video venue within four months, which will give us five morning services.

People are coming each week from thirty miles away in each direction. We have never made much about numbers with our congregation since I came to Sherman Bible. We have used phrases like "We need to make as many disciples as possible with urgency." There is never a weekly report to the church of attendance.

The average person in the congregation has no idea how many are coming to church. We never post attendance numbers. With great humility, I know we are the largest church in our county and most likely the largest in a thirty-mile radius.

Beyond buildings, budgets, and butts in the chairs, there are things taking place that give me incredible joy and energy. Many of those things are measurable, but many more are immeasurable. Our church is growing a heart for people and ministry outside our walls. We have ministries going on each week in public schools through serving the faculty, mentoring, hall monitoring, and being a positive influence to children with dysfunctional homes. Services are being held each week in a number of assisted living homes. Apartment churches are being started. Our investment in missions through giving and teams serving around the world each year has multiplied over the last years. Our financial investment this past year in missions matched our entire income from all sources the first year I was here. We are engaged in helping the poor with food and other services. We are reaching into places that our church did not reach in previous years. We are forecasting four church plants and multi-sites in the next few years. Though we are far from where we could be, this tells me we are moving in the right direction.

The agreement we had eight years ago to be a friend to other churches has started to come to fruition. Partnership in prayer and ministry with over thirty-five other churches of various denominations is taking place as I write. We call it the ONE church movement. Our tag line is "ONE Church, Many Congregations." You can check out the movement at our website, www.churchoftexoma.com. The idea of thirty-five churches (and growing) from various denominations working together in support, prayer and speaking well of each other is unheard of in our area of the Bible belt. God's church working together without competition, comparison, back biting for one great cause of making disciples is a dream come true for me. The potential of this movement is incredible. It wakes me up every morning. I spend hours dreaming and praying for a sovereign move of God in our area.

I doubt if anyone is going to write a book about Sherman Bible Church any time soon. None of the church growth gurus are calling us. So please understand, we have not moved into the stellar realm of mega churches. But it is a humbling experience to know God is doing a good work in a little north Texas town.

When I am asked about Sherman Bible Church from pastors and friends, I report without exaggeration that this has been a great journey. The people have embraced vision. They have given sacrificially in time and money. A guest might decide that Sherman Bible is not the place for them. Our music might be too loud or the casual atmosphere might not be their choice. However, every guest we survey always notes that they sense there is an incredible spirit of unity and joy. We do have an unprecedented unity. The complaints are almost zero. There is an expectation in the air when you walk in a service. I credit that to a clear compelling vision, prayer and people who have grown to believe the church is for others and not them.

You recall I told the elders in the final stage of interviews that they needed a coach and a playbook. In my mind I knew it would be coaches not coach. Because of my biblical conviction of the plurality of pastors and the opportunity that I sensed was ahead, I knew a great team of other coaches would be necessary. In the last eight years we have built an all-star team. If we were in sports, I think we could be invited to the NCAA basketball tournament. You might not think the next few paragraphs are necessary; they are necessary for me to complete my story. I think I have noted that I am focused, a strong leader. Yet, I never have believed I could do anything without others who were exceptionally gifted, had abilities I did not have and possessed an equal commitment to the cause.

I could write pages on each person below, but your interest would not sustain the pages. So here are the Cliff notes on our team.

Frank Sanza: worship and arts pastor. We have worked together over eighteen years. Frank is truly a multi-talented leader. He played football in college and majored in music. He has traveled in theater groups, directed stage plays in large cities, coached high school football, spent some years in the film industry in Hollywood, and has led worship and bands for years. His work and loyalty are immeasurable. He has truly been one of my closest friends.

Jeff Wideman: executive pastor. He was the person that I thought would never come to Texas. Thank God for Billie suggesting Jeff. Jeff and I go back over sixteen years to the church in the Silicon Valley. He is our resident rocket scientist, philosopher and theologian. He is much smarter than I am. I stand next to him to appear smart. He has a PhD in Aerospace Engineering. He left NASA to enter ministry and earned his M.Div. He takes vision and gives it some order and structure. I include Jeff in my short list of best friends.

Drew Svendsen: senior high and young adult pastor. Drew grew up in the San Joaquin Valley church. I have known him since his high school days. He was my first "coach" hired over eight years ago. He has always had a passion for the Word of God in students' lives and has been a rock to our growing student ministry. He is Mr. Steady. Parents trust him with their students. He is not the wild hare youth guy who thinks only of his own territory. He sees ministry holistically. They do not get any better than Drew.

John Davison: middle/jr. high school pastor. John joined our team about four years ago from another large ministry in San Antonio. He is a lover of those students in that critical age group. He is a "get it done" type of guy with a huge heart for kids that bleeds through in everything he does. He is a servant to the whole body, willing to help in every arena of the church. He has rescued many projects we have attempted in recent years. I have to rate John at the top of the class of student pastors. It is an accurate assessment as I was in student ministry for thirteen years if you remember.

Tim Harkins: discipleship pastor. Tim and I go back to the early 1980's. He was a layman in the church in Dallas. He left the business world as a CFO and went to Dallas Seminary to jump into ministry. We snagged Tim from a megachurch in Dallas to come to a little town and a small church. His love for authentic relationships and ministry is unmatched. He is our relational pastor that saves my type A personality. He keeps us focused on people and not projects. Invaluable.

Connie Porter: children's director. Connie left twenty–two years of public school teaching to join us. She made a career sacrifice of reducing her future retirement to be with us. Her teaching resume' and her thirst to execute the best practices make the reputation of our children's ministry the best in North Texas. She took a huge step to join a group of male pastors and has become one of the boys. She is incredible.

Chad Johnson: resident geek, IT and publication director. I could never say who is the most valuable staff member we have, but I know we would be in deep trouble without Chad. We stole Chad from leading the geek squad at Best Buy. He has turned down many job offers to be with us. He could be about anywhere he wanted to be in the job market. He is an outstanding photographer, also. Chad keeps us on the cutting edge in IT, graphics and operating systems.

Josh Tullis: worship pastor. Josh comes from a pastor's home. He has been engaged in church music since he was in elementary school. Incredible talent, a true worshiper, songwriter and boundless energy in worship bring our services alive each week. We call him the "energizer bunny." I also love the fact that Josh looks at music through a theological eye. He sees worship more than the newest sound out. He wants to make sure there is solid theology in the words. This adds value to what we sing each week.

Sharon Barker, Kathy Grove and Jeni Squires: administrative staff. Sharon and Kathy were on staff when I arrived. They have had to adjust to warp speed changes. They work endless hours beyond their pay and have never complained about the abuse we have put them through. Kathy has served on the staff for 23 years. She was the original office person that has worn multiple hats. Recently, she has had to work through her husband's tragic accident that has changed their lifestyles. She has never missed a step and has never expressed self-pity or bitterness. She has been a testimony of grace and strength. Jeni Squires has served in our student ministry for 21 years. She serves in administration and programming. She, too, has championed all that goes on. She adds to the steadiness of our student ministry in a variety of ways. She has a history of girls who were discipled by her. We have others on our staff in our office and interns who serve with the same excellence and passion. They all have been part of a great team of leaders.

I have been a blessed pastor. God has smiled on me with a loving church family and a team of leaders who are far more than I deserve. I did not forget the title of this chapter. I am sure you are familiar with cake mixes and other items that have instructions on the package. Many of them read, "Add water and stir." Local pastors ask me to explain our church with an expectation that I was a brilliant leader, with some complex and powerful strategy. I answer, "The ingredients were already in the package and waiting on me. All I had to do was *add water and stir.*"

Now why did I write this chapter? It was for me. It was for my own celebration of a very kind and gracious God. More than anyone knows, I know I should not be in ministry. I do not measure up to this holy calling. So I needed to remind myself of how good God has been to me. I just have to think that God's ultimate glory is His desire. He does that in different ways. He has brilliant servants. He has His great creation. He has His profound revelation of Scripture and history. Sometimes, as in my case, He chooses the simple, the sinful, and the least among men to show that His work is not dependent on giftedness, intelligence or talent. I write from a heart that is not pure, but is extremely grateful. I write because I know my personal clean ups on aisle 2 should have me out of the race, but God has chosen to let me continue to run.

I write this chapter for you also. You might be one who is weary in the race. You are thinking you have chosen the wrong course to run and God has called you to be the modern day Jeremiah. You have not experienced the shower of blessings in your present situation. I am not going to tell you that the blessings are coming. I do not know. God is in charge of that department. I do want to encourage you to take a deep look at your calling. Do you understand the privilege of being a church leader? Do you really believe you handle precious truth everyday? Have you grasped that God's call is not always about measurable results? God has called you and me to live for the proclamation of the gospel, not the recorded accounting of size, comfort, and man's applause.

I have learned through four different pastorates with four different results that my assignment is God's choice. The circumstances are His allowance. He has assigned me to make much of Him, proclaim the gospel and make disciples. The more I try to manipulate the situation, the more frustrated I become. Hard work, faithful shepherding, and skillful stewardship are included. Yet the smile of God on the work is His choice. (I cannot value the people or myself by the results if I am chasing after His heart, His directives.)

My present post has been the most fun and joy I have had. I do not understand totally. I do know whether we are trying to keep up with the growth or trying to navigate through a cantankerous group of people, I am blessed to be in ministry. I fail when I think I deserve more. I am content when I count each day as a day to discover how God is going to use me in His vineyard. Of course, I love the thrill of what seems to be progress. Yet, I can look back now and thank God for all stages of the journey.

My humble advice to you is to make the day you have a day that glorifies Him. Yes, there could be much better days ahead for you. You might dream of them. You might long for them. But do not let them replace the day you have of being a pastor. The dream of a better ministry or an easier place, can become your nightmare if you are not thanking Him for the privilege of being called to where you are now. God has not lost your phone number or address. He knows how to get in touch with you when He is ready. The question is, "Are you ready?"

I fully believe if I would have come to Sherman twenty years earlier, I would not have been ready. I would not have allowed Him to do what He wanted to do in a little north Texas town. I would have gotten in the way. I would have made another mess on aisle 2. So I say to you-allow Him to do His present work in you today for the future He might have for you tomorrow. If you feel you are the present day Jeremiah with no great record of human-measured success, remember that Jeremiah has gone down big in God's record book. God permitted Jeremiah's ministry for all of us to read today.

Clean Up Assignment

This assignment begins with prayer again. Block out ample time to be with your God and ask Him to give you thoughts and memories of your call to ministry. Go back to why you felt you were called of God to lead. Did it stir your heart? Were you amazed? Were you humbled? Was His glory at the center of it or was your renown at the center? Was it a call to duty or a call to self-identity, public recognition or position of being the front leader?

Now get your pad of paper. Write down what you discovered when God took you back to the beginning.

Look at your writing. Were you honest as you wrote? Is there some realignment that needs to take place? If so, continue to write in an attitude of repentance and renewed commitment for His glory, His plan and your acceptance of it.

Now make a new a page. Write out every good blessing you have in your life, in your family, and in your place of ministry. Write about people who have blessed you, lives that have changed, and undeserved blessings you have.

Now write about your future resolve. What do you desire in the future? There is nothing wrong with great dreams and vision plans. Just be sure they are purely motivated, Holy Spirit inspired and without human comparison. Seek God for His future for you and then rest in His sovereignty.

Chapter Twelve
Passing the Baton

Back in Dallas, I listened to many police officers in the front seat late at night talk about retirement. They would tell me how many days they had left. I have listened to others in other walks of life tell of how they looked forward to playing golf, fishing, and walking beaches. None of those conversations have ever been attractive to me. Today, they are not on my bucket list. I compare this stage of my life to the two-minute drill in a football game. The team is at its most intense effort no matter how tired they are. Similarly, I see it as the last leg of the relays I ran in high school track. I knew my coach and my team were expecting and depending on me to run the best leg of the race. That is why I was the anchor leg. In my anchor lap of ministry, I want to run my best leg of my race. I want to come to the finish line at full stride.

I have come to believe that retirement is an American idea. I don't know if that is true, but I will hold to it. I just can't find a lot of information in the Scriptures on retirement. To me the call of God is a lifetime. Paul's pictures in the New Testament describe the servant of God running hard as he finishes his course. Thus, retirement never enters my mind. It bores me.

With that said, I believe it would be foolish for me to think I will finish the race being an effective pastor of a young and growing church in my senior years. I have preached for years that the next generation should be our focus. We chart the course in our church in Sherman for the coming generations. I ask those my age to put aside their preferences of church style for those that are coming. With age and experience

I try to leverage this for the future. To be true to that vision, I must be willing to acknowledge that a younger leader should be in place and ready.

May I take you back to the relay team in high school? Conditioning and speed work were very important to having four top sprinters on a relay. However, there was another element that our coach knew was equally important. He made us practice over and over the exchange of the baton. We could lose seconds in the race if the baton was not passed with precision. It would be a disaster to drop the baton. The releasing and taking of the baton were critical. It had to be planned, practiced, and perfected.

Churches make huge mistakes when it comes to passing the baton of leadership. There are two main failures I have observed over the years when it come to a pastoral change. One, the current pastor stays beyond his effectiveness. Some stay too long and the church grows old with him. The church loses touch with the next generation. To add to the problem, the aging leader many times tries to hold on to the baton and it is almost wrestled from his hand and is dropped. The second area of failure I have observed is that a pastor resigns and no plan has been in place for his vacancy. There has been no thought given to succession. When a pastor resigns without a plan of succession, suddenly the church is in chaos.

Three years ago in the middle of growth and what everyone saw as success, I knew I needed to lead our elders and pastors into the future. Everyone was elated with the current progress of the church. The present status was wonderful. I knew we had to be strategic and plan for the future. I presented the elders a sketch of a succession plan. I think I caught them off guard. I told them we couldn't stumble in our race by not being ready to pass the baton. I outlined the finding of a young successor that could come on to our staff and run with us, and in the next few years, give him the baton. I did not give them a name of a successor. We basically talked about the type of leader.

After a period of time the elders came back and said, "We think we have a candidate for our team." When they told me they believed the next lead runner should be my son, I was elated. Denny had planted a church at the University of Texas some years ago. It was his second major leadership role. He had led a large young adult ministry in McLean, Virginia, for five years prior to moving to Austin. In choosing him, we were able to eliminate some of the checkpoints on our plan, as he was a known and proven leader with our elders.

In the previous chapter I gave a brief overview of our staff at Sherman Bible. I intentionally did not mention Denny, as I knew I would introduce him now. Being my son, I have to guard my bragging. So I will just give a small sketch. Of course, he grew up in ministry. He watched, learned and thought about church. He was blessed by being engaged with two mega- churches prior to coming to Sherman. His experience with those two churches added years to his preparation. He is ministry-wise beyond his years. He is a gifted communicator, a good strategist and, best of all, has a lot of his mother's traits. I could not have chosen anyone better to whom to pass the baton. My confidence that Sherman Bible will be led well into the future is great. I am a satisfied pastor and a proud father.

We are coming close to the time to pass the baton. The difference between this and my relay team is there is not much rehearsal. The race is going and we have to pass it once. There is no practice try. There are few things written on this subject. It seldom happens this way in churches. Thus, we are passing in the middle of stride and are learning how to do it as we run. We want the timing right. We want a smooth transition. I am sure it will not be perfect, but I am looking at his hand as I write and will soon place the baton in it. I have to admit it is a new feeling. It is hard to pass a baton that you have held for

46 years as the key leader. I am learning and do not want to be the cause of a dropped baton. The wisdom and counsel of elders, staff and my own instincts are all part of the passing.

You may not be a pastor who needs to think about this issue. If you are a Christ- follower, I want you to think about your engagement with the next generation. You may be a lay Sunday School teacher, a discipleship group leader, an elder, church staff member, or public school teacher. Your post is not the issue. The challenge is that we interact with the next generation. It is your job to give them the hope of the gospel. To walk alongside them and give them vision, wisdom, and friendship is your assignment. Tell them of the great works they can do. Tell them that they are important for the carrying on of the message of Christ. Celebrate with them their victories as they run. Come alongside them and guide them to stay on course. Do not separate yourself from those younger. They want a mentor, a mature friend who can give them confidence.

Think of passing the baton to them. As they are ready, then let them run.

Retirement? No! Watch the race from the bleachers? No! So what is the next thing? I will learn to adjust my stride. I will take my place on the team in a different role and allow the runner with the baton to run at full speed. I will change to a role of working with other pastors in our area, training young leaders and being part of our future multi-site start-ups. I will be a pastor to pastors. Will I miss that lead runner place? Of course! However, I am true to my preaching of the next generation. I will run at full stride and support the team. Reality is that my stride is not as fast as the next runner so I cannot hinder the team. Coaching in the final stage of my race will be my new role. Encouraging pastors from around the area and developing with our staff an emerging leaders' training will be my last assignment. I will have the pleasure to watch younger runners develop and be released. I will do my best to stay out of the way of the faster runners and cheer them on to record paces.

I will run with pride as our church spreads its influence broader. I will celebrate as the next generation leads the church to greater works than I ever dreamed.

I cannot know my number of days. God determines that. If I follow the path of my parents, I could have another twenty years on the track. I have a sense of how they will be run. Most of all, I do not want to waste one moment that I have left in the race.

Aisle 2 back in the grocery was an interruption, a minor challenge. It was not a life-changing event. The grocery business was secure, known, and measurable to many degrees. My store manager in my first year of college talked to me about a career in the grocery business. He said, "You could be one of the youngest managers in the chain." He was confident of that. People will always have to eat. "The long range benefits are good," he said, "and you could retire in your early sixties and be in good shape financially." It would have been safe. Looking back through 46 years of ministry, I sure don't want to go back to aisle 2. No doubt, aisle 2 would have been easier, but it does not even entice me for I have been a privileged man to have the opportunity to be a pastor, a shepherd of God's people.

Clean Up Assignment

What is your engagement and interaction with the next generation? Add to your schedule, time to be a mentor, cheerleader and guide for the next generation.

If you are a pastor, spend time looking at your present status. Do you need to be thinking about a succession plan?

Now look at your church. What is the investment your church is making in the next generation? What portion of your budget goes to youth and children?

What appeal does your church have for the next generation? Does your church design its ministry for older adults?

As a pastor do you teach your adults to put themselves second and the next generation first? Do your adults see the importance of investing and programming for the next generation?

"But I do not account my life of any value nor as precious to myself, if only I may finish my course and the ministry that I received from the Lord Jesus, to testify to the gospel of the grace of God." Acts 20:24